Ted on his first day at CLC

Self portrait by Ted

My dad, Ted Schaefer, was a college English teacher. He taught at the College of Lake County (CLC) at the Grayslake, Illinois campus for 37 years. He also taught at the University of Missouri–Columbia as well as Lake Forest College and Barat College in Illinois.

He **loved** words. I can see him now: grading papers on the porch, at the picnic table, and, most often, at our dining room table.

I used to write fake student papers and insert them into his piles as a practical joke. I did this sporadically for close to 15 years.

I never pretended to be a real life student. All the characters and their voices have always been imaginary. My papers are about celebrating students—their unique ideas, personalities and writing.

Above all, of course, the purpose: to make my dad laugh.

These are for you, Daddy.

Self portrait by Ted

Ted grades with Beth

By Beth Schaefer

A funny coffee table book for
English Teachers and the Universe

30 wacky, whimsical student papers
plus **4** hilarious parodies of composition theorists.

Copyright © 2014 by Elizabeth Schaefer
Books on a Whim, Inc. (Evanston)
All Rights Reserved
ISBN 978-0-578-14468-9

Table of Contents

egg·cup (ĕg'kŭp') *n.* A cup for holding a usually soft-boiled egg.
eg·ger also **eg·gar** (ĕg'ər) *n.* Any of various moths of the family Lasiocampidae, whose larvae often construct tentlike webs among the branches of trees. [From the shape of its cocoon.]
egg·fruit (ĕg'frōōt') *n. Botany.* See **canistel**.
egg·head (ĕg'hĕd') *n. Informal.* An intellectual, a highbrow
egg·head·ed (ĕg'hĕd'ĭd) *adj. Informal.* Befitting or having the qualities of an intellectual. —**egg'head'ed·ness** *n.*
Eg·gle·ston (ĕg'əl-stən), **Edward.** 1837 1902. American writer known for his realistic but sentimental novels, such as *The Hoosier Schoolmaster* (1871).
egg·nog (ĕg'nŏg') *n.* A drink consisting of milk or cream, sugar, and eggs beaten together and often mixed with an alcoholic liquor such as rum or brandy. [EGG¹ + *nog*, ale.]
egg·plant (ĕg'plănt') *n.* **1.a.** An Indian plant (*Solanum melongena* var *esculenta*) cultivated for its large edible, ovoid,

Brokeback Mountain Book [Melvin Trodd, Comp 1] 5
When I've Got No Class, I Stalk Famous Celebrities [Barbie Kendall, Composition] 7
Greek Mythology: Surreptitious and Submerged in the Celebrated Series Seinfeld [Sidney Swan, Composition 102] ...9
The Case of the Missing Pupils [Wallace Klempt, Poetry] 11
The History of American Horror Movies: From Tod Browning's GEEKS to M. Night Shamalamaham's THE SICK SCENT [Törsten Kelp, Comp 2]..12
RED PEN ALERT: This document is CLASSIFIED: A Choose Your Own Misadventure Paper [Annis Theesia, Anguish Composition] 16
Kaffka's The Fly, and Cronnenberg's "The Metamorphistufs" are totally GROSS [Chilton Goods, Short Story]..18
Burrr… There's a ~~Breeze~~ Draft in Here [~~Lenny~~ Lenard Blum, Compasition 101] 20
Is this Advanced Primate Psychology? I think I may be in the wrong class [Chianti Bouteille, Advanced Primate Psychology (?)]..21
Invasion of the Faculty Snatchers [Percy Patton, Creative Writing]........................24
Tenureless Voices: An Awe Filled Lot of Adjuncts in America [Transcettia Mirth, English] 26
Stuffed between Heaven and Hell: Is Taco Bell Are Savior or the Devil Incarnitas? [Jewel Cardot, Compozition 101] 29
King Kong Steals Professor's Pay Day and Ascends Vending Machine [Hugh Redditsch, Poetry] 32
This Paper Contains the Origins of the Universe –Literately [Lincoln Topper & Epiphany Dunno, Journalism]..33
I Will Not Let My Willow Weep [Sarah Charles, Creative Writing]..37
My pHd is fur the Sabbathical, not the Celery [Hilly-Rae Lime, Comp 1010] 38
The Intrinsic Quandary of Unionizing Interns [Sam Serriff, English Composition].................................41
On Auragin of Theses [Helen Stamford, Ph.D., Poetry]..............43
Hall Bell Has Broken Loose! Has Anybody Seen Alfredo? Or: The Alarming Tale of a Missing Exchange Student [Cherry Black, Intro to Playrighting] 44
Astroprojection in the Classroom: A Credit-Wurthy Feet [Mary Maladies, Composition 100] 48
Java Script: An alarming report on the direty for coasters in computer labs [Morris Cold, Newswriting]..50
Teacher, please intradouche me 2 hot girl in the 1st row?? [Jeremiah Toed, Compt 1 o 1] 51
Pinocchio Malwired: The Leftover Secret Code [QWERTY Keys, Comp 1]..................53
"Time Outs" Made Me A Better Man [Donnie Muhwee, CLC Composition 102]........................54
From Stall Secureity to the Hippo Campus: How to Make Collage a Better Insditution [Nora Lane] ..56
The Little Engine That Couldn't [Yolanda Docente, Fiction 3].................................60
I Treat Bell So Well; So Why is my Fairy so Myphed? [Tilly Woods, Fairytails Class] 62
My mom wrote this paper. I'm so embarrassed. [Icy Thicket, Comp 1] 64
Professor, please hold me back after class! The mob in the hall is closing in on me! [Ana Mona Pia, Comp 102] 67

Featuring the Presidents Playhouse

TERM PAPER

**The Nutty Years of the
Jon Stewart Presidency in a Nutshell
(2012- 2016)**
[Edison Bell, Composition Class] 70

COMPOSITION THEORIST PARODIES

Edifying the Heads of the Student Body by Means of Application of the Romance Languages as a Didactic Discipline of the Composition of the English Tongue
[PETER ANKLE].. 94

Extrapolating the Fundamentals of Dexterous English Composition By Tutelagical Virtue, Endemic to Asian Languages and Chinese Symbolism
[DAVID BARFHOLOMAE].. 97

Bad Ass Drafts: An excerpt from Tail by Tail: Some Instructions on Writing and Vibes
[ANNE LAMOTT APPLESAUCE] 101

Make No Room for Kids: Bells Ding for Online Classes K-8
[An Argumentative Abstract by RICHARD FUKERSON. Sponsored by The University of Phonics] 103

CHEEP SHEET

This book is laced with whimsicalities:
random plays on words
random people—real and unreal
random events—actual and fictional
random references to movies, books, theater, art
and random randomnesses.

The "Cheep Sheet" sheds light on each paper's playful remarks and references... 107

Peter Ankle

David Barfholomae

Anne Lamott Applesauce

Richard Fukerson

booksonawhim.com

Melvin Trodd
Comp 1
11-30-2009
Prof Schaefer

Brokeback Mountain Book

Brokeback Mountain is a movie and a book, and the writer of the book, Annie Proulix writes that the movie is a very great representation of the book she wrote. I completely agree with her because the characters Ennis and Jack are in love even though both men are men which makes the love on a whole new level. I hope it's okay I chose this book to review.

In both the book and the movie the men share intimate moments on the backs of their mountain. They have intimate moments on each others backs and on their own. So the title the name of the mountain and their love affair are all a pun intended. The fact that Ennis rhymes with a bad word is no coincidence, but the point is that it's okay so long as you are true to nature. Their love is rocky like the mountain, another metaphor.

The subject of homosexuality is a phenomena that predates back prior to the date Proulix wrote the book in 1963. But Brokeback Mountain simulated a new genre of gay short stories which made it to the big screen and in the end to the red carpet. Heath Ledger won a posthumerous academy award two years ago after his death. This shows that the movie is as good as the book.

Both the movie and the book take place in Utah with trips in different states like Texas. The fact that the mountain lies on the border of Wyoming and Utah is not a coincidence because the theme of crossing the border surfaces again and implies the gay race.

Just like in the movie in the book the first homosexual man Ennis marries his wife. In both publications this shows that love can conquer in the end. She loves him and feels sad when he dies even though they broke up.

Jack is a cowboy who rides cattle in the rodeo and wins sometimes if he is a lucky strike. He married to a rich woman played by Anne Hathaway from the Princess Bride. In the book Anne Hathaway is not a lead actress, but in the movie she is. Both Jack and Anne are in a holy good relationship, but Jack misses Ennis and men in general.

It is a similarity that in both the movie and the book Ennis and Jack meet again regularly each year on the back of the mountain. And they love each other in both the movie and the book. They just love each other longer in the movie.

In my review, I like this movie but I cannot relate to the characters because it makes me a little uncomfortable but I support them. I believe I related to the book because it did not give you with the mental images. I respect Annie Proulix for her masterpiece and Lee Ang for his masterpiece.

Barbie Kendall
Composition
Professor Spaefer

When I've Got No Class, I Stalk Famous Celebrities

Since as long as I can imagined, I'm fascinated by movie stars.

I used to climb fire escaped to roofs to gaze at the twinkly lights of Los Angelos sparkling on horizon behind my hometown's Golden Gaze Bridge. I beamed at the constellations twinklying above LA, memorizing-and-connecting-the-lines. Yet I did not see them as tigers, Orion and the-lion-that-looks-like-a-mouse. In the constellations I saw Erkel, Stamos, and the-Night-of-Bell-Air. When Home Alone, I'd gaze at the glow-in-the-dark star stickers on my bedroom ceiling and see Mackulay.

So, I herd through the grapevine at that hospital on Hollywood & Wine {San Fran branch} that-when-I-was-born the delivery man proclaimed "a star is born to stalk"! My late mother {that's how she knew she was with child} says what he really said was "I'm doing this ad hoc". {But she was anistonsized, so her hearing wasn't hearing cohearantly.}

My first Target was a child-kid star. {Perhaps your great-grandkid's kids have herd know of Justin Timberlog.} Justin lived a convenient 5-hours-and-51-minutes from San Francisco to Los Angelos. {Or a less-easy 34-hours-and-56-minutes if you abbreviate LA and take I-40.} So, naturally the-first-place-I-drove when I turned 16 was HollyWood to see Timberlog. It was a taxing bus ride but better than the long run. Later I'd learn to claim it.

I buyed Timberlog's street address from *WE Magazine* with my return-bus-fare. So, it was like this: Justin was on-his-corner, I was in-his-street. It was perfect, an Idol opportunity to address him. I-remember-to-this-day that I-don't-quite-remember what he was wearing. But he wore sunglasses.

Than it happened: Justin removed his sunglasses as I waved hi! on the hi-wave. He waved his hand back at me as-if-he-was-shoeing-a-way-a-mosquito from his face. Those diamond eyes! Wow, the impact they had on me! {Those cars really hurt}.

Such a rush (!) it gave me that rush hour. But, back than Justin was only like a Bozo-Clown-Club star just-smacking-puberty with Spares. From that point-of-contact on, I went pro: It was union actors only. {Justin was born in Florida like Mickey only later.}

More stars followed {always men cause I'm not}: Keanu Reeds, Johnny Drip, Wellwater Phoenix, and the-son-of-Tom Hanks-and-Maria Shriver.

So, it's spicy because they all have, like, different reactions. Sometimes they run: Sometimes they dial three-numbers-on-their-cellphone or their agent: Sometimes they just act bored and stuck up—like they think all-the-sidewalks-of-the-Universe has their star or something.

booksonawhim.com

But, sometimes their nice and flutter their eyes at me like Justin-but-without-the-mosquito. For example, even though I'm not old, I once stalked Jason Bateman. Let's just say he didn't arrest MY development! *Nudge Nudge.* In fact, he didn't have me arrested at all. That was nice of him.

Jason was nice, and we got close in a proximity-kind-of-way which was emotional for me. I was about to call a pizza-delivery to get my-foot-in-his-door. But when Jason stepped outside in his bathrobe and slippers, I knew I wouldn't have to place that order. Jason spotted me and I came out from under the bush. He smiled, gave-a-little-wave, picked-up-his-newspaper, and turned-to-go-back-inside. Than he thought better and turned back to look at me again. He opened his mouth, and I'm sure he was about to invite me in or something.

SCREETCH! Just than his sister (another Justin) sped-into-the-winding-drive screaming at me, flicking me all her ten fingers: brandishing a gun: screaming me to vanish. Jeesh Justina {!}. I think she was jello that Jason made it to the big screen. Probably her guns a prop from one-of-her lame made-for-TV movies. Sadly, I had no choice but to flea.

Anydoodles, I moved to Grayslake, Allinoy when I herd their was a Major in Voyeurism. Plus Spielberg filmed The Breakfast Club at CLC. So, maybe someday Emmanual Estavez would come to CLC to remise about his hi-school days when he felt Shiddy.

But it's past 12-months now, almost a year {!} and I STILL haven't-spotted-a-star. In fact, I only took this class because your related to hotty James Spaeder from Pretty in Pink. Than I noticed last week you spell Spaeder with an F. I've Goggled Lake, Cook, and McHenry County men stars. All that comes up are lame fogies like Adain Quinn, Charelgun Heston, and who the hell is Jeremy Piven??

It's not that I don't like your class, Mr. Spaeder, but this-hole-Midwest-stint Bites-the-Bullet and I miss shoeing them away. The MINUTE I get my Associates, I'm packing my bads to give New York City a shot.

Other cheesy stalkers wait-by-Broadway shows stage doors to-get-a-glimps. But me? I take the hi-road. Me, I'll be hiding in the mens laboratory stall at the famous-fancy-restaurants stars go to at midnight-after-their-shows.

My stars won't know what hit them when I spring {!}.

It's anticipatory as waiting for a shooting star:
Swing doors swing open. Swing doors swing shut. First footsteps. Zipper {zziiiipp}. About to exhale.
Than, when I hear that famous tinkle, I'll get that inside tingle I live, and may someday, die for.

Assignment: Describe a piece of art (book, film, show, painting, photography) that has deeper meaning than what is portrayed on the surface.

Sidney Swan
Composition 102
Professor Schaefer

Greek Mythology: Surreptitious and Submerged in the Celebrated Series Seinfeld

Even the noblest and most civilized of American TV academics are blind to perhaps *the most blatant* example of subliminal messaging in the history of domestic sitcoms. Seinfeld, allegedly "a show about nothing," is, on the contrary, the antithesis of such a proclamation. Throughout the duration of its lifespan, an impressive ten years, the television show boasted light banter, twisted humor, double entendres, outrageous and eccentric characters, impossible wagers, daring quests, brash actions, theatrics, sex, and romance. Sound familiar?

While the origins of Greek Mythology date back far farther than the summer of 1989, when the pop hit piloted across the Peacock's perky network, in its perpetual nest at 30 Rockefeller Plaza, the similarities between the loveable likes of the Seinfeld colorful cast of characters and the off-the-wall shenanigans of the Greek Gods are uncanny. The cacophony of New York City traffic is not unlike the brazen clamor of the centaurs tromping across Mount Pelion. And it's not the background noise alone; the funky bass notes between the scene changes in Seinfeld echo the lyre, similarly a stringed instrument, created from the entrails of bovine.

From the tall metallic glimmer of Manhattan skyscrapers to the glistening palatial peaks of Mount Olympus, all kingdoms need a father. So cometh forth **LARRY DAVID**, our **ZEUS** among men. Just as David materializes in several Seinfeld cameos, so doth Zeus among his assemblies. Both are the ultimate writers of all transpirations—moral or meaningless. Either one can pull the plug or change the scene at any given time. The audience and the entire cloak of civilization are at the mercy of their four powerful hands. Seinfeld fans across the nation applaud the scenarios, and in the magistrate of Zeus, all gods rise in his presence.

How the TV public does not see this analogy off the bat escapes me. For example, in one Seinfeld episode, David appears as a grouchy vendor at a newsstand *(Season 7, Episode 10)*. This is glaringly symbolic of Zeus's cantankerous delivery of bitter news and punishment. In another cameo, David cries out "Look in the sky…the planets are on fire…like flaming globes!" *(Season 2, Episode 8)* which parallels Zeus's command that Atlas carry the sphere of the sky. David also regularly graced the set with his voiceover impersonation of George Steinbrenner, the owner of the New York Yankees. While David lends his voice to Steinbrenner, Zeus's booming voice reverberates down to the Games of Olympia.

This leads us to our protagonist, the namesake, if you will, of the show: **JERRY SEINFELD**. Before I even utter typographically his Greek doppelganger's appellation, it's likely already on the tip of your tongue. Yes, **DIONYSUS**. "The God of Merry Making, Theatre, and Ecstasy." Just as Dionysus is a child of Zeus, Seinfeld —a stand-up comedian and lover of women—is a brainchild of David, Seinfeld's creator. Seinfeld is depicted as a successful comedian; his fame metaphorically channels Dionysus's golden chariot. Like Dionysus, Seinfeld is a protector of those not belonging to conventional society, in particular his rascally cohorts George Costanza, Elaine Benes, and Cosmo Kramer. Another parallel: Dionysus was especially attractive and popular with the nymphs, albeit it in a caregiving capacity. And, while in the real world the perception of Seinfeld as sexy is up for grabs, in *the TV show* he plays quite the ladies' man. Dionysus was born on the island of Ikaria. A true New Yorker, Seinfeld was born on the island of Manhattan. Just as Dionysus debases the oppression of the powerful, Seinfeld refuses to succumb to conformity and never sells out. Need I go on?

At this point, you probably needn't I reveal that that laughable, self-loathing, miserly sidekick **GEORGE COSTANZA** mirrors a certain, shall we say, **SILENUS**. Silenus, of course, was the faithful companion to Dionysus, and they reveled together in their wine and merry making. And while we never spy Costanza visibly inebriated, in "The Betrayal,"*(Season 9, Episode 8)* Costanza deliberately gets Benes drunk on peach schnapps which alludes to a tendency for abusing spirits. The resemblance is not sheer suggestion: Costanza and Silenus share common physical traits as well, such as baldness, squat nose, short stature and pudgy belly. And while Silenus has the ears, tails and legs of *a horse*, similarly Costanza has the behavioral characteristics of *a donkey*. The dead giveaway that Costanza is Silenus embodied is in "The Phone Message"*(Season 2, Episode 4)* in which Costanza sings "How do you solve a problem like *Maria?*" If you listen very closely, you will hear he sings, "Medea" not "Maria." This makes perfect sense, because Costanza is played by a Jason A., and *Medea* and *Jason of the Argonauts* had an extremely contentious relationship laden with problems.

Soar we now to the beloved **ELAINE BENES**. Our eternal **ARTEMIS**. Artemis, the "Goddess of the Hunt," daughter of Zeus and sister of Dionysus. While those who ascribe to the Roman Orthodox myths call her *Diana*, it was *Homer* who references her as Artemis. Thus coincidence it's not that "The Simpsons" precedes "Seinfeld" weeknights on Fox. Artemis is fabled to be totemic: the emblem of the young virgins whom she yearns to protect. This may bring to mind "The Virgin"*(Season 4, Episode 10)* wherein after unwittingly embarrassing Seinfeld's then-girlfriend—who as it so happens is undefiled—Benes fruitlessly attempts to comfort the fruitful chaste maiden. Indeed, one of Artemis's pleas to Zeus is to bring light to the *Trojan War*. This is only logical since Benes' favorite method of birth control, the sponge*(Season 7, Episode 9)* is being taken off the market, so while the average TV viewer might assume she'd opt for the somewhat similarly-positioned diaphragm, Benes is full of surprises. So my gander is that it's more likely she'd turn to Trojans. You may also recall that Benes coined the term "ya da ya da ya da." Or *did* she? English/Greek translators will find it no coincidence that this catchy expression—which persists well past the show's grand finale, is "ναι da" which is Greek for "God bless you."

Finally in saunters **KRAMER**, a spot-on depiction of **PAN** if there ever was one. Before delving into the psychical parallels, let us glimpse the tangible resemblances: Pan, of course, has the hind legs of a goat. Zeus's lightning bolt splits people in half. Although human flesh, Kramer is symbolically half goat from the waist down, as supported by the *frizz in his hair*, resulting indubitably from the electric shock *Zeus's lightning bolt* caused. Pan also boasts horns and he is often linked to sexuality. If you threw Dionysus, Silenus, Artemis and Pan into a room and challenged them to a bet of self-indulgence abstinence, who do you think would succumb to horniness first? Right. I can tell you've seen "The Contest"*(Season 4, Episode 11)*. Pan also is known to nap aplenty. Remember "The Friars Club"*(Season 7, Episode 18)* when Kramer takes 20 minute cat naps every three hours. The *ultimate* proof that Kramer emulates Pan is quite literal and symbolic: In "The Apology"*(Season 9, Episode 9)* Kramer cooks a steak in the shower. And to cook a steak indoors one needs, of course, …you said it, a pan.

All good things must come to an end…and all bad things too. In Seinfeld's very last show "The Finale"*(Season 9, Episode 24)* the crew of four is condemned to *a year in prison* for failure to be good Samaritans. Specifically, for turning a blind eye to a man in need. If the cast is metaphorically monstrous and only able to see with one eye, are they not the one-eyed *Cyclopes* sentenced to *Tartarus*, the dungeon of the underworld?

Will Larry David rescue Seinfeld as Zeus rescued the Cyclopes? It depends how you look at it.

Wallace Klempt
Poetry
Schaefer

The Case of the Missing Pupils

I. My students' pupils appear to be missing
Their palettes of irises glistening
But where is that spot?
That dilating black dot
As I lecture, I'm not sure they're listening

II. The whites of their eyes still intact
Their sclerae, to be exact
Those who drank beer before bed
A few streaks of red
Like male cardinal eggshells that cracked

III. They don't blink; they appear unperturbed
It's the pinnacle of my talk, are they stirred?
They don't seem to care
They're slumped in their chairs
Are they visualizing my every word?

IV. The matter about which I lecture
Is the nuance between fact and conjecture
My dear little matriculations,
They're missing my gesticulations
Should I enlist an intern to act as inspector?

V. I debate, should call 911?
"Teachers shan't play Father" is *my* rule of thumb
They don't seem pained or insecure
Do they see black or a blur?
So I teach on, and project to their eardrums

VI. I hope sightlessness doesn't precede their demise
Like Piggy in *Lord of the Flies*
I aim to glean their collective insight
But their corneal sheens give me a fright
There's so much to be said in the eyes

VII. I wrap it up; has their interest been piqued?
I invite questions yet not one doth speak
Motionless as if under a spell
Yet they rise at the bell
We'll see if they come back next week

TÖRSTEN KELP
Comp 2
Prof Spadefür

The History of American Horror Movies:
From Tod Browning's GEEKS to M. Night Shamalamaham's THE SICK SCENT

My mind's eye spots bloody horror like a clot. (I get chills, but they satisfy me.) When my mom stopped nursing (red eye shifts), I sated my hunger by feeding myself bedtime stories from *Videodromnuts* (1983), *Time-Warp Orange* (1971), *The Texas Coleslaw Massacre* (1974) [went well with *An American Werewolf in Onions* (1981)] and *Hollow Weenies*—all 8 seasoned.

Horror movies were invented by Arson Welles, the first American director to practice the culinary art of fleshy guts. With *Citizen Pain* (1941), this trailblazer set fire to Hollywood with his chilling tale of an old man on his deathbed who is trying to confess to the gruesome mutilations he conducted forty years before: Slicing off Christmas carolers' noses with the sharp, detached blades of his sled, "Noseblood." But the nurses just keep bringing him tissues, and the old man dies of exasperation. While *Citizen Pain* brought him acclaim, Arson was fired by the studio after releasing a touch of evil on the set, and his envisioned sequel, *Citizen Insane*, never came to light.

Although Arson claims first directatorship of bodily gore, Tod Browning takes the stake with his innovative stab at "Reality Horror" with his deranged and sickening *Geeks* (1932) *Geeks* features a cast of real life nerds—social outcasts who are ridiculed and ostrich sized. Garbed in big dorky glasses and tight suspenders, the geeks mobilize to brutally tar and feather the captain of the cheerleading squad. This may call to mind its successor *Feathers* (1988) starring black sheeps Christian Slayer and Winona Knifer, when the outcast young lovers peer-pressure the feathered-hair popular girl to drain a Molotov Cocktail in the kitchen.

For some reason, probably an unreasonable one, high schools in America often serve as movie backdrips for bloody ruckuses. Take Carrie. (I can't stand her.) Carrie is the telekinetic in Brain Dead Palma's high school horror flick *Carry* (1976). The end of the movie is gross. Carrie wins prom queen and as she's carrying her flowers on stage (in front of pretty much the whole school) a pretty Mean Girl pulls a rope that dumps a bucket of REDRUM on Carrie.

AWKWARD. Bedlam ensues and spiked punch floods out of the cracks in the elevators' door frames, filling the gymnasium—drowning students & chaperones with rum. A living hell for the cleanup crew and designated drivers.

Blood can really stain a rolled out red carpet, but black and white stains are harder to wash off your brain. In Psycho (1960) there's one scene I can't scrub off with all the bar soap in Arizona. The scariest sequence: Kathy Bates strips naked singing in the motel's shower, and the proprietor-in-drag slinks in with a plunger to unclog her pipes. [In the same cutting-edged vein, there's a wicked black and white movie called The Blair Witch Project (1999) I'd like to cite. But I think it's foreign, not American, because it was filmed in the woods.]

Throughout horror movie history, it's common to see old horrors molten into modern day horrors. For example, the Three Faces of Eve (1957) that's about a psychologically deformed lady suffering from multiple personality disorder. Her one head contains three faces—each marvelously played by Joanne Woodchip. Eve's faces are horizontally aligned, but because they share one throat, they have to take turns talking. On top of that, Eve must wear her hair up in a bun or else she'll get hair in her mouths. This classic was incorporated into the modern day horror flick Seven (1995), in which, as a closing sequence, Eve's 3-faced decapitated head makes a surprise appearance in a hatbox.

Not all sequels follow decades later. In the spirit of Starved Wars, (1999-1977) sometimes the sequels are filmed first! Consider Adolf Hitchcock's To Kill a Mockingbird (1962) and The Birds (1963). **The Birds** is, in fact, the *prequel* and stars Tipping Headless as the San Franciscan socialite who saves a small Northern California town's children from evil birds' attack. In the sequel, **To Kill a Mockingbird**, the birds remobilize in the South and Atticus Flinch, played by actor Gregory pecks back at the birds; first terrifying them by shouting "Boo!" and then killing them with his pointed teeth and poignant performance.

I have to say, I can stomach carrion just fine, but what I can't stomach is people (dead or alive) EATING carrion. And unfortunately, this is a common theme in horror movies. The first authentic zombie movie was Night of the Living Dead (1968) in which about a half dozen humans shack up in a farmhouse to ward off flesh-eating zombies. The sequel, a film adaptation of the Broadway musical production of Sweeney Todd (1982), whose musical numbers include: "They're coming to get you, Barber" and ""Nothing's Going to Eat You, Not While I'm Around."

Characters Mrs. Love It and Todd (no relation to Browning) kill customers who then turn into zombies and eat the two lovebirds. Like in its predecessor **N.L.D.**, the zombies consume the entire cast by the end. In the finale, the zombies eat Mrs. Love It on a bun to the catchy tune "ba da da da da...I'm Lovin' It." [The subjective influence of horror flicks on fast food and commercial marketing could be a whole paper in itself.

Yes, corporate marketing and political propaganda play a surreptitious role in American horror movies. Not surprising, some of Hollywood's biggest producers are Toy Makers and The Republican Party. This is Blairingly evident in The Exorcist (1973) **The Exorcist** contains such shameless subliminal messaging from Mattel promoting the agility and limberness of its Malibu Barbie (box date: 1970), as demonstrated by possessed demon child Regan (!) whose head does not pop off when it twists around at a 360 degree angle.]

There is another prominent theme in American horror movies I haven't mentioned. CHILDREN. According to most horror plotlines, when it comes down to it, CHILDREN are the ones to fear. Two of the freakiest child terrors flicks are The Brood (1979) [which is Canadian, that Canadians would argue is a part of America] and Children of the Corn (1984) [which is Nebraskan, which Nebraskans would also argue is a part of America.] [Another horror masterpiece hails from Northern-most America- Dead Slingers (1988) starring Jeremoany Irons as twin arachnid gynecologists who torture a black widow, sublimely played by Theresa Russell who splays her eight legs with graceful apprehension.]

Eek...The little terrors in **The Brood** are genderless, mutant children who murder anyone their institutionalized "mother" is disturbed by, and from her they are born from a grotesque external womb. Yuck. Similarly, the children of the corn follow the orders of their leader "He Who Walks Behind the Rows" which is a clear threat to anyone in the cinema scared to get up to leave. The scariest child of them all is, hands down, Rosemary's Baby (1968) in which a sweet, aspiring mother bears the baby of Woody Allen, who he proceeds to kidnap and eat with sage.

Another theme in American horror flicks is EVIL NEIGHBORS IN SUBURBIA. In Fright Night (1985) a middle-aged studly dude, who's really a vampire, attracts sexy women in his lairs [his house] and bites a hooker's throat as for played by actress Heidi Sorenson (July 1981 Playboy Magazine's Playmate of the Month). Disturbia (2007) is a newish cinematic endeavor to paint suburban neighbors in a creepy hue. In **Disturbia**, a teenage boy spies on his next door neighbor [played by David Remorse] through binoculars and determines Remorse's a serial killer because he has a dented car and a screaming ladyfriend houseguest. But the next morning, Remorse pulls a Dressed to Kill (1980) by wearing a wig to make it look like she's leaving the house to throw off the neighbors, while under the assumption that a man in a wig is less conspicuous than nothing.

Another suburban thriller is Consenting Adults (1992) in which a crazy perverted neighbor man "Eddy Otis" propositions another perverted (but not crazy) neighbor man to a wife swap deal that results in murder. Yeah, a suburban block can seem All American and clean-cut at the start of the movie, but soon it all goes to the dogs. In Pet Dreams on Elm Street (1984), [Tagline: "Whatever you do, don't maul a sheep"] a teenage girl has nightmares in which she's trailed by a vicious, fanged sheepdog named Freddy Cujor.

The WORST horror movie ever made was Gigli (2003) starring "Beniffer" Affleck and Lopez. Affleck plays a mobster armed with an embarrassingly bad accent; and the disambiguation of a corpse's thumb in hand with the attempted suicide of Lopez's lesbian lover solidify its position in the horror genre. The horrific performances earned the disaster flick an astonishing six Razzie Awards including worst movie and worst performances. This set a new record, beating It Happened One Fright (1934)—starring Darth Gable—which took home five Razzies in 1935, including Best Stalking Picture.

Now the BEST horror movie ever: The Sick Scent (1999) by M. Night Shamalamaham. [A genius moviemaker with many a blockbuster before him.] It's about a ghost and a boy. Spoiler alert: When we find out—at the end of the movie—that the ghost this kid has been consorting with is actually ALIVE and DECOMPOSSING, it's quite startling. ("I can bear smelly people.")

It makes you think back on all the earlier scenes where you were SURE the ghost was dead: When sitting with his wife at a fine dining restaurant. She pours her glass of wine on his head. WE THOUGHT it went *to* his head because he was a ghost and couldn't hold it. But no, it went *through* his head because of the hole rotting through it. SO yeah, the character DIDN'T die in the first scene, but was slowly decomposing throughout the entire film, which explains why near the end of the movie everyone is holding their nose. (It's only similarity to Gigli.)

I hope that my snapshot of American Horror Movies has been thought provoking for you. Now, bedtime...Lights out.

Annis Theesia
Anguish Composition
Professor Schäfer

Wed. 2.22.1995
Subliminal Messaging: Don't Fail Me Now

RED PEN ALERT: This document is CLASSIFIED
A Choose Your Own Misadventure Paper

So, Ted,⋯can I call you Ted? We're grown-ups here. By the way, my name is **ANNIS**. **A.N.N.N.I.S.** (Don't think I don't know that you don't know my name because I know you don't).

Do you notice my combat boots that kicked ass in Kuwait? **No.** Do you notice my black braid I zip into my armoured-skirt? **No.** Do you notice my tassels *East Berliner tank? (*West is for Wussies). **No.** Have you noticed I switch into German now and again wann auch immer ich will? **No.** All Annis is to you is another name on your class rooster.

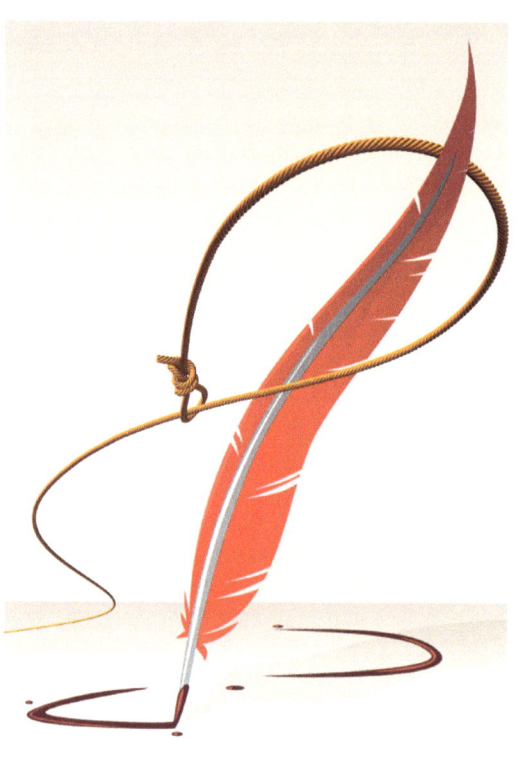

Now Ted, here's how this's gonna work ▶ Your gonna put that eager little red pen of your's back inside it's saddle, and corral the little puppy back to it's pen. Red classifys me as a "Loser". STOP arresting my confidence: I WILL NOT wear a scarlett "L" on my forehead. !

This assignment *write about your greatest adventure*. Well my paper is *your* adventure, Ted: choose your *own* adventure:

If you decide to slather my paper in red ink to make it a Grade F paper, go to A.

If you decide to lather my paper in stars to make it a Grade A paper, go to F.

A.
You awake every morning at 3:15 AM. Bedridden with evil ideas. You will rise out of bed to rid your brain of these evil coaxings. But one mourning you will suckthumb to the evil and fetch your ax. I won't reveal the horror action you will take, but here's a clue: look up the difference between an ax and a bull in the *dictionary* or *National Geographic*.

If you still decide to fail me, go to D.

If you change your mind and grade me a A, go to F.

B.
All of you're students in all of you're classes turn in plagarized papers for the REST of you're career. You are convinced the papers are plagarized but all the students and their parents all go to the dean and he says to pass them any way. You will be forced to give the plagiarized papers all A's and shoulder their parent's smug smirks.

My paper is the last authorentic paper you will ever read.

If you still decide to fail me, go to C.

If you change your mind and grade me a A, go to F.

C.
The brain cell that checks coats and takes names in your left brain will immigrate to your right brain because he hears it's a hell of a lot more fun over there. So he leaves his post and joins the right brain party with the imagination, crazy painter cockedtail partys, foreign movie sub titles projected on your graffiti covered cortex, stereos cranked up and bottomless pits of Schaefer beer. This means you're brains left side coat check is unmanned. You're curse is you will forget the names of you're students, you're colleagues, the clerks at the copy machines, you're neighbors, you're not so distant relatives, you're⋯oh wait. Your left brain cell coat check guy already immigrated⋯?

Whatever. In any CASE, you have chosen your path. Go to H.

D.
You will grow a green mole, a small bump that oozes watery puss eturnerly. The mole will live on the southern-centermost tip of you're nose like a upside-down lime snowcone clutching the slope for fear of falling or being snorted into the abyss. Tissues and surgery will not extract the mole. The rest of your life your students will mock, pity and revulse you.

If you still decide to fail me, go to B.

If you change your mind and grade me a A, go to F.

F.
Good choice Ted. Now that you're sense is common and you've laid that little red puppy to rest, you will awake every morning refreshed, invigorated, freshly showered and smelling like Irish Spring, and the sun will always shine in your eyes. You're students will be equally alert, energized, itching to write, Carpet Diem flowing through their blood, and they will never raise a hand when you nod off.

My Assignment: Choose a short story that was made into a movie. Read the story & then watch the movie. Compare the too.

Chilton Goods
Short story
Prof. Shafer

Kaffka's *The Fly*, and Crownenberg's "The Metamorphistufs" are totally GROSS.

I like reading short movies and shorter stories so I was glad about this assignment order. I was going to compear and contract "The Man Who Mistook His Wife for a Gnat" by Oliver Slacks with Carole King's *Flea to be You and Me* but Carole Kane's was a play with songs, not a movie.

So I went to my library for my furst time to rent *The Fly* by Franz Kaffka and the book too. The book is called "The Metamorphistufs" which means something like contaminated bugs in computers but at least it is in American even tho the title is Russan. The movie *The Fly* is a movie about a fly. It was directed by a woman director named Franz which is like how they say Fran where the movie takes place because the actors are American or really good. The actress in the movie Gina Davis is a woman too. But she doesn't play the part of the fly I think all flies are women so that is one giganic oversite of Fran. I don't think I can support women who say there should be more women directors and this is why.

In *The Fly* takes place 13 years ago and the "The Metamorphistufs" takes place over one 100 years before then. The "Metamorphistufs" is so old it takes place back when London was still a city in America before it was destroyed by the plaque. So the contractions between the two both are very different because they were filmed in different decades. The actor in the *The Fly* is Jeff Goldblum. He plays a scientist named Seth. The actor in the "The Metamorphistufs" is named Gregor and he was written by Dan Crownenberg. Crownenberg wrote the book so many wars ago his book is posthummus. But he probably knew he was liked.

The contractions between the furst scenes are as unalike as can possible be. I mean in *The Fly* the scientist is talking out at a party with Gina Davis and in "The Metamorphistufs" the scientist is a salesman hermit in his locked bedroom too shy too go too parties. Jeff Goldblum doesn't discover he is a fly until near the end of *the Fly* after he gets Gina pregnant but they had sex when he was a fly to so the baby may be a fly so they are having a girl. Gregor doesn't have sex in the book even though he has a cleaning lady and a sister The sister Greta is sweet until she betrays him like a sister wood. The cleaning lady fights Gregor with a stool when he attacks her so it's a relief she's fired at end. Gregor dies before having babies. But that is probably for best. He would probably eat the baby eggs because his sister stops feeding him all tho when she furst knew he was a fly she did feed him milk. But he didn't eat her food until it was rotten.

Differences are the movie is in color and the short story is in black and white. The movie fades out and in with a lot of gross body parts falling off and insect legs sprouting out of Seth's toresewn. The book doesn't fade but the words on the pages sometime turn to white sooner when it's the last page before the next part. "The Metamorphistufs" has three parts and The

Fly is one long part without intermissions since the batteries in the remote died. I thought watching the movie furst will help me like like the short book better But they were so different it was like having to be made to watch two different movies you don't want to see twice.

There are not many similes between the two. Both men are flies. Both plots have instruments in both plots. Seth plays the piano and Gregor's sister plays the chello.   There is violence like Gregor's dad throws pears at him and Gina Davis shoots Seth. There is a similie's that the two flies are grotesk. That's how revolting the flies are and both flies made me sick. The part where Jeff Goldblum pukes white acid and sucks it back up again was so gross made me actually puke too. But my puke was some pop corn I ate when the movie started. Jeff pukes all over like an exploding vaccuum but mine was just a spot the size of a roach on the rug so I didn't need a vaccuum to suck mine.

Even though you can't see the screen in a book, the sickening scenes in "The Metamorphistufs" book are even grosser then seeing it for real in *The Fly* movie. It's not hard to forget Jeff Goldblum but I can't escape the graphick images Crownenberg inprinted in my brain at each page's turn. The movie grossness just made my eyes sick but the book grossness made my brain sick and I can't blink a brain to swat away the memory.

The creepiest parts of "The Metamorphistufs" is when Gregor is scuttling in circles up walls and he hangs upside down on his slimey legs. When his mom spies him on the ceiling she faints she's so cowardly. Gregor gets all filthy from neglect and emancipated from not eating enough from Greta when she shows her weakness against her brother's. It's not Gregor's fault but it's a relief when he dies. It's a relief when Jeff Goldblum dies too but he dies different then he dies in the book. In "The Metamorphistufs" Gregor dies by choice just like suddenly magically In the movie Seth dies by choice only after his failed attempt to fuse his decaying mutated body with Gina Davis and their fetus into one person in his telepods. He is a genius inventor but Gregor was a pitiful salesman.

There IS a big blooper between both stories that is a totally gross oversite. The two flies DON'T FLY! Jeff Goldblum leaps good high and crawls up the walls but he does not flap his wings and fly And Gregor Samson also skittles about but he too DOESN'T FLY. I am not surprised that Fran didn't think to add it into her movie because she's a she so she's naturally short sited. But I am surprised that Dan Crownenberg did not think to write about this common practice of a fly into his story Maybe Dan is short for Danielle.

Period.

~~Lenny~~ Lenard Blum Assignment: Write about your favorite season
Compasition 101
Professor ~~Ted~~ Schaeffer *(sp?)*

Burrr… There's a ~~Breeze~~ Draft in Here

My favorite seasin is the spring bcus it's a time of sonny breezes that flutter *(filter? Can wind filter?)* into my moms kitchens window that's mine to. My mom used to had a padio in the backyard when we lived in Okanomowok. *(Note to myself: check sp and if it's a Native Indian American name make sure you say that so you sound smart to teahcer But don't use word Indian !!! bcus that's racist and we killed the Indians when we were Vikings from the Santa Maria (cruise ship)tho we gave thanks @ the Last Supper on Thanksgibbing)* At spring on the padio we listened to bird chirps laying eggs in the tree trunk like an elephant. *(< Good! Assimilie!)* There had been a daddy bird but he flown south for the summer like daddy birds do. *(mention dad? No gawkward ,,but he DID go to Tallahassee and that's south so it clever to inclood)*

Spring is the beautifullest time of the month. It cymbalizes rain, Buds, Light, flowers like tuleps, turnips, and peeonknees. I herd from my 8th *(6th?)* grade teachr Miss Cellaneous *(Mr Erieous?)* that people who live in French celebrate spring with Maypoles—alltho that is a contradickshon in terds bcus spring starts in april *(double check)* and Poles don't live in French. A ledge Ed Lee *(who the hell is Ed Lee???Ask mom, dont say hell tho)* the French pop corks off bottles of wine to wring in the spring *(good alliterdation!)* with cheer *("and beer?" Cheer/beer   Like the rhyme, but I don't think french drink beer (thats germany or milwakuee)but teach prob wont know he's from Wilsonsin)* and beer

The only problem with spring , in my apinion is FLOODING and TAXES. My mom says taxes are the worst and they start spring, it's on the calender But I told her some taxes have floored-weel drive and drive-thru flash floods fined without getting clogged. We live in a cul de sack and it floods alot bcus it's under ground. To bad it does't not flood in the winter bcus then we'd go ~~rollar~~ ice skating! *(Good!)But now my favorite seasin seems like winter I'd have to erase the part about the French in milwakee but I COULD keep the part about Vikings eating with Santa and Madonna Magdelyne)*

(Lenny lissen to your self make sure you include the details about visual details and emotions Schaeffer lechers about) Spring colors are pink and yeller Trees get green like after winter hybridnation. Pine needles grow back and birch and asprin trees are no longer white with snow. The best about spring is the feeling of freshly mooed wet grass between my slippery naked toes. ~~H~~Jose cuts our grass for no taxes mom says, so I guess ~~H~~Jose prefers landscrapping to driving people between airports. When the grass leftovers *(moss?)* is dapper from rain, I floss my fleshy toes with ~~twigs~~ sticks. Then I "leaf" *(grate play on worms!)* the wet stinky clumps in my liddle brudder ~~Sammy's~~ Samuel's sandbox.

In climatology, spring is defined in the Northern Hemisphere as extending from the vernal equinox to the summer solstice; the temperatures transition from winter cold to summer heat only in middle and high latitudes; near the Equator. *(~~Source: Lake County Visitors Buro.~~ Is this plagueism? May be teachr won't notice Sounds good keep in Dont feel bad Lenny ur good persn Now end paper I'll say how odder seasins suk to make spring seem bedder)* Fall is to scarin Trees fall off and you have to rake them up. Plus naybirds look scrary in masks like 2 marry farmers w pitchsporks in painting. *(Good! also farms in ~~f~~Fall and farmers ~~F~~fall in love)* Summer hot: I get sweatery and I do not had fire hidrent for splashing like kids in rural *(like the country)* America *(like the country)* Winter is to tire-ring bcus I can't stay a wake til 12pm to into the Nude Year even tho I can. But spring is best, bcus of the warm sonny breezes that filter

(Note to my self: use spellchex on computer for 2nd versin, & burn this draft)

Chianti Bouteille
Advanced Primate Psychology
Fall Semester, Week 5
Professor Schaefer

Is this Advanced Primate Psychology? I think I may be in the wrong class...

Your class is really fascinating. How primitive mammals don't make eye contact. How ancient man shrugs and slouches to act out a Neanderthallic evolution from sedentarily hunched torso to a stooped arched stand. The moaning sounds the primitive humans make like when they are in heat or digesting. I am taking avid notes, and I already feel smarter just by being here and sitting tall and thinking. Thank you.

But it's Week 5 and we still haven't examined primates. Yes, we have covered **Cro-Magnon posture, dialect, and cognitive detention** to a great degree. I appreciate your **Gestalt psychoanalytic role play method** to teach ancient mammalian psychology by means of observance. That's really cool. My favorite cognitive takeaways so far are your—almost chemistrial—manifestation of how **semantic memory** gets soggy when it neglects to absorb reason; and the **ancient oratory enactments** when the role player stands up to address the class. Ingenious, so creative too!

And you gave a grand demonstration of **the holes in avoidance learning** by awarding an A to the brilliant thespian in the first row who feigns trouble-making in a crude tongue. Clearly an undeserved reward will not circumvent a mammal's innate lust for mischief. (Playing a little game of **operant conditioning reverse psychology,** are we?) No matter how unpleasant the situation, the monkey in us all will keep monkeying around. Bravo for a fine and original impartment of wisdom onto us!

I rested assured momentarily in Week 3 that I was in the right class when I spotted the hairless-faced boy with white spotted cheeks and his girlfriend with the dyed patch of black on her head—mashing their heads and lips together in the back row in a blatantly **apelike simulation of passion and violence.** Their fists—clutched in each other's—appeared disjointed as they thrashed their hands about the other's neck in carnality.

What a show! I connected the dots: They were depicting **Freud's notion of the innate, primal ID** in action; enacting sexual and aggressional urges unrepressed. Of course! And the dislocated hands surely a sign that **the lovers were emanating gibbons,** whose two traits of uniqueness lie in their monogamy and disjointed wrists allowing for biaxial movement when swinging.

But my hopes were dashed when the hairless-faced boy's wallet slipped out of his pocket and spilled its contents on the floor, which included a driver's license, a tube of Chapstick, and a student ID that identified him as a native of Ohio, not India or China where bona fide gibbons roam. And the world knows, of course, that **natural selection wiped out the dry-lipped gibbons** 2 million some years ago due to their inability to suck the juices out of fruit for sustenance. Besides, if primatal, what would the boy need a license for? Gibbons are arboreal.

The supreme confirmation that the unabashed lovebirds were not playacting exposed itself in the form of an 'I Heart (romance symbol) Mom' tattoo on the male's deltoid which I spied as he leaned over to collect his strewed belongings. At first my heart leapt…you were orchestrating a parallel between **Freud's Oedipal complex** as repressed by the monkeying male!! But everybody knows that gibbons are monogamous, so that theory went squat.

So the uneasiness reversed back to the pit in my stomach. I search for other signs that I am in the right class. I'm gathering knowledge and hunting for clues.

Is **free association** your pedagogical method? My **hunter/gatherer technique** has produced mere straws at which I'm clutching. Let's see, free association = **psychoanalysis:** apes on couches…there are couches in the student lounge. Typically, hung-over or overly studious night owls occupy them unconsciously… Mountain gorillas dwell in cloud forests in the tropics at canopy levels…Does this signify that gorillas suffer mental unrest due to i**mproper bedding, water binges or nocturnal diligence?**

Clutching clutching clutching…

What if this is all a sublime enactment of **prosimian cognitive dissonance theory**? The environmental conditions to generate cognitive dissonance must be highly motivating. This course, Professor, is motivating to say the least. It's provoking my every mental cell to decode the multi-fascinated layers of fact; play; innuendo; and common sense occurring on this class—or rather stage—room floor. Now, in cognitive dissonance theory, the pool of subjects must have conflicting thoughts which may be counterintuitive with the **subjects' voluntary actions**. (Now why am I telling you this!)

So…Week 4's group writing fiasco comes to mind.

When you divided us into small groups to write about our summer as a **collective whole**, I had that familiar sinking feeling. How do summers concern primate psychology? The classmates in my group commenced, throwing random words out like "skateboard camp" "pot" "this is lame" "sleeping in" "bikini beach baking" "I forget" "Dairy Queen" "summers with mom" "weekends at renaissance fairs"; etc. I threw in my own "audited an intensive pottery wheel therapy workshop" for the sake of formality and conformance. Plus…my interest was piqued.

Here's where the conflict comes into play. When our group finished our essay on our collective summer, the renaissance fairgoer did the honors and read our paper aloud in an unconvincing cocky accent. He then made a very strong statement about the right to wear armor at school. My fellow group members were visibly agitated, I not excluded!

Our essay had not included such a political, controversial statement. But **our allegiance was with our peer**. Should we dissent, he would be chastised, heckled, maybe even flogged by means of flunking. Should we not object, those of us adamantly against armor on school property would be betraying our conscience. This supports **Leon Festinger's theory** that a **belief disconfirmation paradigm** exists: As peers we rationalize why we do not intervene when we realize we should.

Which, as I think of it, *does* symmetrize with **chimpanzian social behavioral theorosis**. "We have the choice to use the gift of our life to make the world a better place--or not to bother," according to **primatologist Jane Goodall**. Her point being, that chimps are blessed with a gift to knuckle walk on all fours. It is a trait they may use to the betterment of the entire chimp population. It provides them with a speed and agility to save the young from predators, and extinguish fires fasters with four buckets at once.

Yet, there is a **sharp dichotomy between the two chimp species socially**, and that's where the group writing exercise may factor in. The common chimpanzee will exhibit **antagonism when socially challenged** by defending its territory—mental and material, whereas the Bonobo chimpanzee shirks confrontation by **incessant love making**. By not standing our ground and speaking up against armor on school property, we were essentially making love to each other like the Bonobos in cowardice.

Yet to produce cohesive actions as a result of communal thoughts, a primate's cognitive reason must be transmitted through **subglottal pressure and laryngeal air sacks**. Philosophomoric novelist **Ayn Rand** said, "Reason is not automatic. Those who deny it cannot be conquered by it. Do not count on them. Leave them alone."

Her profundity may be applied to the orangutan community. Orangutans are the most intelligent of the primates. Second in line only to humans. So Rand's point may be, although orangutans are intelligent, they may not automatically abide by their wits. If they stand up for what they believe in, they may fail and cannot be relied upon. This may shed light on the orangutan practice of, when annoyed, **blowing air through pursed lips**. These are likely the orangutans that are holding themselves back from voicing an opinion.

Unless, of course, you've cleverly added a twist to this, and these simulations of vacuity actually are symbolic of the **free-thinking primate**…That we, human beings, in the most literal sense, are primates. What an excellent parallelism! I applaud your brilliant technique! And somehow, despite the clues, I'm still reluctant…

As I'm hunting for understanding, I'm gathering you are playing the role of **perceiver**, and I as **judger**. How splendid! I know you cannot break character, but I really need confirmation. Am I in the wrong class?

Nod once for yes. Nod twice for no.

GOODALL **RAND**

Percy Patton
Creative Writing
Proffessor Schaefer

INVASION OF THE FACULTY SNATCHERS

The night is dark and stormy. A raindrop falls from a cloud mysteriously and spins stoplessly on a sidewalk that has no cracks yet from students steps. "Who!" coos an owl. Could the owl mean "who" like a human? It sets tone for students scared to go inside the school. The torrential downpour is at a school on a campus. The students go inside because they have to. Why are they feeling so scared? "Why!" coos the owl. The rain rains down harder than the hardest rain in historys past. The garden pods look slimier and shinier than yesterday...

When the students entered the building that looked like an office building. It was a night class so the halls are darker than torcher chamber. Footsteps from the rain were the janitors nightmare come true. The nightmare for the students are inside the classroom doors. "Open!" "Who said that"? the students read each others minds. They are the fortune tellers of the college.

They know they have no choice on earth but to open the doors and sit in class. Creeekk. The students flow in their classrooms like a river. They sit at their desks. One has a knife scratch into its wood with initials and a heart like a true lover tattoo. An arrow pierces through the heart makes the students heart beats faster. That red marker dots are may be drops of infectious blood. There is lightning flashing outside the window that makes the panes look cracked. Was the slimy ivy there last week peeking in like a curious worm? They know. The students are the fortune tellers of the college.

The teachers have their backs facing the students. No they are not being rude. Something is terribly wrong inside them so. They start to shake their shoulders and the students shake fear. Why are the teachers backs turned and shaking? Shake shake shake. Like electric shocks in their skins. Train cars chugging up down their spines under their skins. Ribs in their backs jutting like tracks in thin skin. Little bumps popping out. Why won't they turn around and teach? They stand like if they statues but they are statues getting electricuted.

No don't turn around!!!!! ···But they do. The teachers turn around in unisson even though they're not together. The students jaws drop and hit the floor.

The teachers heads are mucky. Their faces scooped out like a pumpkin with a sharp spoon. Their necks look like tree stumps without trunks. Their organs are gone its only skin. The teachers skulls and ears where their faces used to be. They have no eyes or brains. Their skulls are an empty gunky fish bowl.

"ATTACKKK!!!" screamed the faculty through their throats without mouths. And the teachers stretched out their arms like Frankensteins and gurgled and walked around. Pandneumonia ensued. Mayhem ensued like little sisters that wants to be carried home. "HUNGRYYY" screamed the teachers and their necks drooled boiling ooze.

The students were smart. They collected themselves in a circle and were scared. The smart students said ideas like throw a stick and run in opposite way and throw books at their faceless heads. The dumber students cried or pretended it was a bad nightmare. Student in each class took out a bag of potatoe chips or baby carrots and distributed the artillery like guns "Ready! Aim! Launch! Fire!" The students threw the snacks real fast at the revolting teachers.

"GRROOAAANN! MOAANNN!" the teachers groaned and moaned. Their arms are still stretched out and they start walking into walls like they are bumper cars. There are pieces of their tongues and nostrils and foreheads all still flapping on the floor. But where did their brains go? Bump into this wall. Bump into this wall. They turn around and groan some more walking into the next wall and the other. Sometimes they are bumping in windows that break their skulls chips.

The bold students ran from the rooms down the stairs and into the elevators like a fire alarm. They ran to their houses or apartment apts. or nearby shops and stories to take cover. But the torrential downpour magically transformed into a drizzle. The students were safe.

All the colleges students rose up the next morning curios. Should they go to class or should they stay home sick? What if the teachers were still wanting to eat them and had scooped out gory faces still? But they had found new found courage so they went back to school like as if no invasion happened.

They entered their classroom doors. Their teachers had their faces back and were facing the class. The students sat and took attendance: Eyes. √ Nose. √ Mouth needs wiping still oozing. √ Cheeks. √ Chin. √ Brain...Brain..?

"Where" coos the owl. Brain. Out to lunch. Don't check.

Transcettia Mirth
My research paper
Professor Shaefer

Tenureless Voices:
An Awe Filled Lot of Adjuncts in America

Abstract: 3 triangles against multicolor streeks of white paint with necklessed heads rolling downward defying gravity and a cow on a roof eating graded cheese in his hoofs playing an octagon violin with a toothpick.

Thesis Statement: Adjunct teachers inherently possess an institution-manufactured awakefullness that makes them be happier, better teachers.

Introduction: In 1976, a brilliant Professor Udon from Flamenco University-- Fayette, Utah (F.U.F.U.), vetted 27 fresh, ambitious pups of pedant-degree. These young, fresh-faced English graduates, embarking on their 1st college teaching jobs, were fresh-faced and young. Udon tracked them threw out the next 20 years, monitoring their anxiety levels and graduationill pulls with magnets; and probing their static electricity. Udon invented EASY (Electrolyte Anervusreck Stability Yinyang) to measure their nervous and school systems beating in vitae. Udon interviewed the adjuncts as they aged regularly. I've Xtrackted Xcerps of his study to support my paper.

My paper starts now:
27 (twenty-seven) of the fresh graduates were willing to be scrutinized *au gratin for the sake of intellectual. By 1996, 3 (three) had won tenure; 6 (six) were teaching full time untenured; 8 (eight) were teaching as PT adjuncts; 1 (one) was teaching as PE adjunct; 4 (four) discovered new careers all together; 2 (two) reached theological Zen; 1 (one) reached philosophical Zen; and 3 (three) went missing and are presumed missing. My paper highlights the 8 "Class of '76" graduates—no longer young, but still fresh-faced—adjuncting part time and loving it hour by hour.

Melba Wry *(Columbia University, Miss)* Comp Teacher
Wry is a rare-bred; she was pronounced tenureless at age 29. She attributes her tenurelessness to the late hours she Xhausted with the late Dean Donald, assisting him by spinning bottles and tales.

Mantra: "My students are my children…if I fear for them, they'll fear for me."
Proud adjunct for life: "I embrace my freedom. I'm flitting hive to hive, eating my bread and honey. Missouri-U has been my 'on again off again' for 20 years; they grant me the luxury to take off whenever and whatever I want."
Consensual student agreement: "We love that Wry doesn't bristle when we come to school baked."

Hugo Oguh *(Hopkins University, Baltimore, MYLD)* Creative Writing Teacher
Oguh is very vane in panes; he peers at his reflection in windows alledgedly. Oguh was granted tenure in 1984. But was stripped of it in '85 when he was caught lap dancing during an aquatics class.
Mantra: "Even if you dive young, never deny yourself the thrill of living the fast lane."
Proud adjunct for life: "It was either that or prison."
Consensual student agreement: "Mr. Oguh sometimes doesn't speak in class but lurks in the corner or bangs his head against the wall; so you can zone out without fear of reperconcussions."

Roger Stallion *(UM-Ann Arbor, Michgan)* *Modern Lit Teacher*
Stallion is known for his electrifying eccentricities like igniting fires by flicking his thumbs, swallowing oyster crackers speared with oyster forks in flames, and lecturing on stilts in a kilt.
Mantra: "There's no I in Teachng."
Proud adjunct for life: "I never applied for tenure, I knew they'd say no. I figured if I stayed part time, the Chairmen would let me keep doing my act."
Consensual student agreement: "Stallion is really weird, but he gives us A's when we clap for him, so he's a'aiht."

Annie Peacepenny *(Chapel Hill University, NC)* *Poetry Teacher*
Peacepenny is renowned across the Carolinas for herself published work: "The Moon Goes Down on Yesterdays."
Mantra: "Literary geniuses know that the plural of genius is geniusi."
Proud adjunct for life: "Tenure is a myth. I'm not one for conspiracy theories, but the other day I swore my dean dangled a carrot cake in front of me, and whoever heard of cake on a pole?"
Consensual student agreement: Ms. Peacepenny devotes entire classes to her book signings, and awards extra credit for paying her complements. Pretty much all we have to do for an A is buy her book. Buy her book online, you don't even have to show up."

Paige Turner *(University of Buffalo, NYC)* *Journalism Teacher*
Turner's fearless courage has secured her status as Iconian in the cafeteria. Turner notoriously interviews studential stampedes as they trample atop her. She won the Pulitzer's Clearinghouse Prize for her investigative article: "A chef's dirty secret: The *real* reason chopped celery makes tuna salad crunchy."
Mantra: "It's not about the subject; it's about how you RAISE the subject"
Proud adjunct for life: "After sustaining so many injuries under the brigade, I felt Adjunctinism would give me the freedom to cry. We cry because we're nobodys. But without tears, we're nobodys. So this makes us somebodys."
Consensual student agreement: "Turner's screwy as all sheol but easy enuff to flip thru fast."

Wong Invet Mint *(Barkeley University, San Francisco)* *Liberal/Martial Arts Teacher*
Mint, once a Liberal Arts teacher, karate-chopped his way into the Athletics department to be taken seriously. Purportedly, Mint did not find the Doonesbury comic strips tacked on the Humanities bulletin board as riotous as the rest.
Mantra: "I've nothing against liberals, but it's the art that moves me."
Proud adjunct for life: "Students bow before me in class. If I were tenured, they'd be kissing my feet undignified. Humph. I'm having the part-time of my life! Who could ask for anything more?"
Consensual student agreement: "Not that there's nothing not wrong with Wong, s'that it's weally wong to wonder."

Fay Lee Unst-Haybell *(Bloomington University, Indianna)* *Linguistics Teacher*
Unst-Haybell was a triple major in English, Band, and English Bands. However, after losing her voice, she pursued a career as a linguistic teacher in the mid-1980't's. She designed a hip new class: "Intro to Tongue in Cheek."
Mantra: "It boils down to this: linguistics or linguini; it's your choice. I choose to eat."
Proud adjunct for life: "'I've got the whole world in my mouth.' I sing it proudly in my shower on the days that I do."
Consensual student agreement: "While it would help if she talked, it doesn't really matter since the class is about derivations and stuff."

Conclusion:

My paper illustrates the institutionalized alertfullness and awakefullness that part-time adjuncts possess.

My paper supplies the quotes supplied by students as supplied by Professor Udon who interviewed them to support my claim. I couldn't have done this without picking Udon's noodle.

20 years of research plus one week (Udon's + mine) conclude adjuncts are alert and alive with *Carpe-hourem*. How do they do it? Easy!

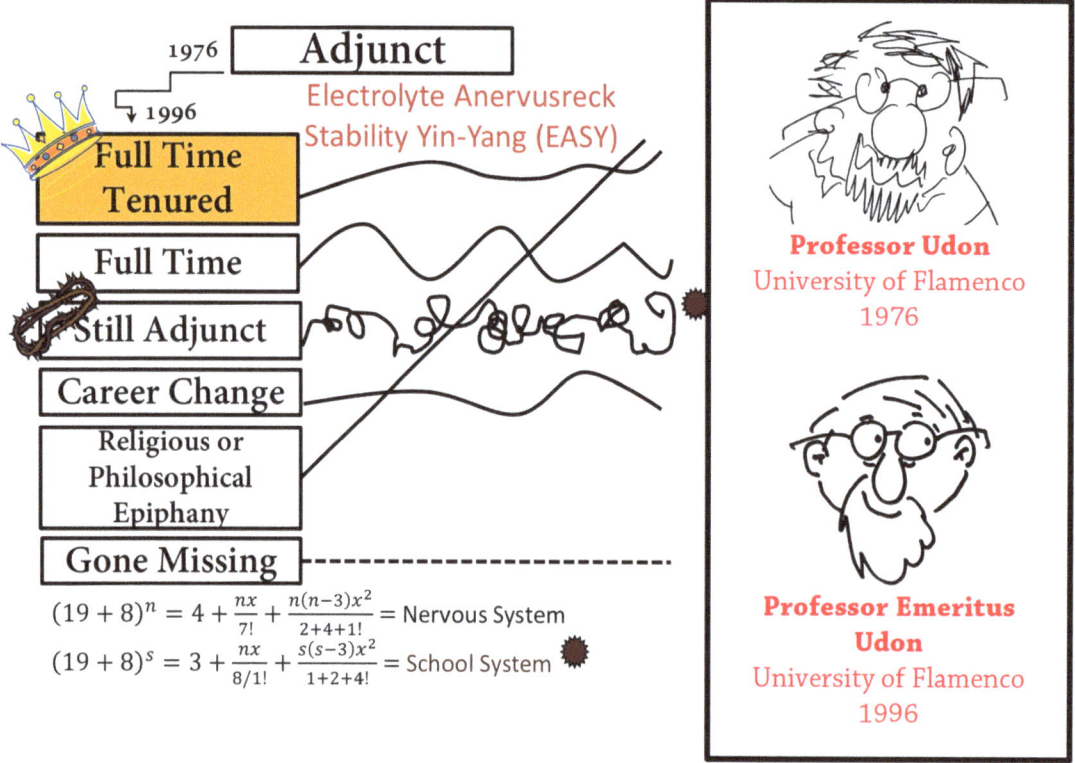

$$(19+8)^n = 4 + \frac{nx}{7!} + \frac{n(n-3)x^2}{2+4+1!} = \text{Nervous System}$$

$$(19+8)^s = 3 + \frac{nx}{8/1!} + \frac{s(s-3)x^2}{1+2+4!} = \text{School System}$$

* *means for free*

Jewel Cardot
Compozition 101
Profesor Shaefer

Stuffed between Heaven and Hell:
Is Taco Bell Are Savior or the Devil Incarnitas?

Ding dong, Taco Bell, you had me at Hello. My first taste of Taco Bell was at an IHOP on the corner of Circle and Ring. It must had been almost dawn because it was after bartime and the sun sets in the south. That's a metawhore because Mexico is in the south when your coming from north America. And I am proud americian but I respect hispanik border jumpers because my boyfiends dad comes from Texas and hes' always bord and hogs the remote when Im over.

I wasn't with my borfiend that night at Taco Bell because we broke up befour we met. And this was befour we met and I was with my big sister Dominic Cardot but she marryed last winter in Veil, Collarado and her new last named is Saint-Nick.

I was maybe 19 with fake ID so they let me in IHOP after many beers. I didn't look like my picture of girls face with hair because Im a frosted blond and the girl who was 21 was brunet unless her ID was fake too. But the waitress didn't check because I ordered 7Up and pancakes. Or maybe it was Spite and French tost. I drank to many beers to remember.

Dominic said This sucks and I want a Maragrita. She wanted a margarita to but with sugar on the brim. [We poored salt on the table and totally laughed off are ashes.) Butt I wanted something with cheese like nachoes. I asked the guy at the booth behind me and he grunted something like Go to Hell and I said thanks I never tried that but I seen the sign. So Dominic and me forgot to pay the bill and left to follow the sign that was lite but not flashing like Girls Girls Girls or the bowling alley near my dads. Dominic thinks her dad is different but that depends if and where are mom lies.

A smelly guy in a big coat and mittens without fingers opened the door for us which wasnice but then he slammed and said something like rhymnes with sheep steak and gave me the finger in the middle. Dominic said we were supposed to give him money and I felt a twist of guilt but I spended all my money at IHOP.

It was really freezing out because it was winter and we live in the middle of west.When we went inside Taco Bell and got a whiff and I screamed. Now I know why the kids call it Taco Yell, and why the guy without fingers that wanted my money was smelly. It's a good thing about inheritage I was born with strong 'Towel or Rinse" my mom says which means I can wash bad smells right off of me with napkins with out showering.

My stomach stopped beating in shock when it looked up all the choices at the menu ceiling. Menu had nachoes, ksawdeeahs, burritoes, beans in bowls ("smoking" Dominic said funny), Mountain Due and even tacos!!!! Heaven I told Dominic. Were in heaven and its not just cause I was high [but don't tell CLC principel. I don't want to get dispelled).

There was two kinda cute guys behind the counter that totally looked Americian or from the dells. One was doing homework or some kind of notebook sheet. Totally lame, we wanted authentick Mexician for the ambivalance like bullfighting capes and sombraros and umbrella toothpicks that open in Maragritas (alltho it doesn't rain in Mexico). College boys probly from univarsity. Thier rich parents probably pay for thier rent, but Dominic and me live with are mom so were luckier becus we don't pay nothing. The other guy looked tired but stood up straight so maybe he was the manager or janitor or something.

But we were there for food, not boy candy, so we ordered hard Shelled tacos and juicey burritoes whose beans kept squirting out and I ate my nachoes with oozing orange steaming cheese. We were only having pretty much pennys and a couple crumbled dollars, so we shared are Mountain Due. We used 2 straws so it wasn't gross and were sisters so it doesn't really madder. If the food was Heavan, my sister was the angle. There IS life after breath.

We sucked out the beans that were squirting out of thier flowery tortiyas and Dominic laffed so hard she spit hers out. Most got on my wet tray but some spitty beans dropped on my nachoe. To be funny I ate it and Dominic practically exploded like a totally cracked up bomb.

Then I laffed cause her face got red and she said it's full of salsa and she puffed out her cheeks with air and she look life that fish at the tanks at the field trip. Then Dominic put her inside of her hands on both of her cheeks and press in flattening her cheeks, pukering her lips shooting out salsa which it really was! Salsa splattered everywhere even the wall like a tomato soop in my microwave.

I laffed so hard that nachoe chese spray out my nose. Dominic clapped her hands over her head like she was applausing at a metal band or baptissed church or something. 'My sister is AWESOME" she screamed and stood up on the booth table in her leather boots which were wrecked from the snow and Mountain Due.

That was like the ultimate complemend I never got. My boyfrein NEVER tells me "my sister is AWESOME" and neither do my littlest sister Aldie, but maybe that's cause Aldie is 1 and only says "goo goo" and 'poo poo'. Plus I only see her every other week end so I don't expect her to know Im not a neighbor.

"Look Jewel I'm surfing" she said one footon each of the handles of my tray, balancing like she riding the waves. I gave her the surf sign with my two fingers, but she looked down at stopped laugh. Her mouth dropped open it was empty but would have been funny if it wasn't. "What Dominic? Miss a wave"? but she didn't laugh [That hert}but stepped off my tray and the table and got down on her nees on the floor looking at her tray that still had food on it.

"It's him she said." I looked at the food on her plate. A couple beans in cheese, two nachoes, a ksawdeeah, two cinnamen twists. "It's Santa. Look."

Holy Quacamole. She was right! It was Santa she was right. Pointy triangeler ksawdeeah beard. 2 pinto bean nostricles. Curly nachoes ears, cute and scrunchy. I reached to grab a cinnaman twist but my sister slapped my left hand and called me a sack of religoats. She told me they were Sanatas eyes I asked why do it madder?

"BECAUSE HE SEES US." Dominic said fattily. "He knows what youve been eating and he knows if youve been good."

"Does he nose his nose is running?" I totally cracked up at my joke. "Look at the cheese under his pintos."

I thwart Dominic will say "My sister is AWESOME" again, but no she got mean mad and slapped my other left hand harder then when she slapped the right.

"Be respectful. He knows we are a wake. Listen, he's telling us something." Shes smart with hearing voices from the other side, so she switched places with me and put her ear to his nachoe, then she remembered that was his ear, so she put her ear to his beard. I asked Dominic what he said. I didn't tell her Santa got his earcheese on her ear. She might slap me again that herts my feelings more then my hands.

"He says to follow his beard." We both looked at each other and are eyes were like big bare moons with red lightnings. Then we looked back at Santa, and the tip of his triagulating beard pointed out the door. It was fate because that's exactly the second a minute later the janitor manager said it was time to go they were closing. We left Santa there on the tray in a trance.

The smelly guy was gone from the door, but we helped him lock the door from the inside. Where was Santa's tip directing us to? We musted follow the clues. The beard had pointed out the door of Taco Bell at an angel that we turned to. YES. We saw it. Kentucky Fried Chicken. Smack dab there be four us and there was Santa again on the sign. This time he wore glasses and a little bow tie and red stripped apon.

They probably don't open til noon or 12 or something I told Dominic. "Isn't Xmas worth waiting for" she asked me but not really because she didn't let me answer. I didn't want to bust her bubble (I'm conscious when I want to be). Besides I like they serve mashed potatos like at grandmas but homemade.

So we are waiting for KFC to open. It's cold but Im with my sister. Then we'll find the next sign inside KFC. I see the smelly guy waiting at the door too. I'll let him open the door for me and Dominic, but I won't give him my money.

HUGH REDDITSCH
POETRY
PROFESSOR SHAEFER

A student's soliloquy straight from the teacher's mouth

King Kong Steals Professor's Pay Day and Ascends Vending Machine

Quarters, nickels, and dimes, OMG.
Change is spared, but not sense, inside these robotic walls within school halls.
A Pay Day bar: The last of its kind. Now we're paid in ACH's. Ashes to Ashes. Rust to Rust.
My candy is stuck in descent, in the grips of metal rings like claws without nails.

I am a teacher with tenure. So why is my pay day bar in purgatory?
Stale on the inside. Sticky on the outside. No, I am not talking about myself. Am I?
I stare at it, snatched. It won't budge. I didn't budget for this. I can only stare and imagine.
Wrapper slightly ripped where its butterfly wing corrugates like miniature waves in motion.
Ah, a vacation… When does my candy bar expire? Does it matter?

DIIINNNGGG. The bell. What happened to the music that was once to my ears at that chime?
It's taken a toll on me. No, silly. Denial is the best medicine. After chocolate…
Floor tiles tremor beneath a million little marching feet:
"Gotta get here." "Gotta get there.""Rush Rush Rush Rush"
Me, I just want my Pay Day bar. With my eyes on it as the mass pass by me.
Embarrassed to shake the machine, but craving conquers dignity.
Shake. Shake again. Still stuck. Call Student Services? What to do…what's that?!?

A pounding. A pummeling in the hallway. Bang! Thud! Boom! Thump!
What animal could this be? The children, as they are to me, have already nestled into closed doors.
Dear God, I see the beast. It is inside the school. It's a gorilla. A monster.
A…I don't know what, but it's BIG and STRONG. It pounds its chest like a big bass drum in a parade.

The gorilla lumbers over to me, stomps, and stops at my side. Sympathy? ROAR!!!!
It hoists up the vending machine, mightily shakes it high above my head, and my Pay Day tumbles to the bottom tray. The beast slams the machine back down on level ground, punches through the One-Way PUSH swing doggy door (explains the bones), and snatches the candy I inserted coins into slits for.
Hmmm. A millisecond pondering distraction – my brain flits from one fear to another:
My pension is now pennies. The vending machine does not accept pennies.
Wake up! Back to reality. The gorilla in the room!

The mammoth monkey climbs the vending machine, His giant head crams up against the ceiling.
He peels the wrapper off my Pay Day bar like a banana, tearing into the candy bar with a fierce, primal chomp. Chump. Have I got chops?
The chimp spits shards of hard toffee like fragments of shrapnel. They rain down on me bruised.
It's an art. Teachers are artists. We're resilient.
We persevere in this Sweet Scary Life.

Reporting in Tandem Assignment ☺

Lincoln Topper *& Epiphany Dunno*

Journalism *1-oh-1*

Professor *Teddy Bear* Schaefer

Journalists' Forethoughts
While I comprehend the craft of tandem reporting—most notable example: Bernstein and Woodward—I fail to subscribe to the theory that better knowledge may be gleaned from co-reporting. Tandem reporters must be assigned <u>discriminatingly</u>. Writers should be paired with their comparable cognitive counterparts. Tandem reporters must possess a civilized command of language, literacy, and logical reasoning: Especially in an article as paramount as this. – Lincoln Steed Topper

Im excited to write about the auragin of how mother nature borned us! - Epiphie

---

This Paper Contains the Origins of the Universe --- *Literately*

Tuesday, March 3, 1998
Camden, Maine

It's a crisp, cold morning in Camden. Sea gulls are shrieking in the awakening air. There is a wafting scent of hot coffee from a stand. You can taste salt crystals in the still sleeping wind. An old man in a knitted, latticed-like shawl wilts over a bench by the seaside—tousled locks of seaweed strewn askew across the wet sand. The two young journalists—one keen and invigorated, the other alert with vacuous peppiness—meet at the beach house and, armed with questions, approach the old man.

Linken told me we were going to find the porpoise of the universe!! He paid my plane tickette to Maine and was super nice. Still I wished the seats hadn't sold out on his train. It would be haven to sit with him for 26 hours talking about our class assignment and picking his coconut. Wish his B&B had had vacencies, but I like my holiday inn express!

The young journalist and his companion were ecstatic when a local jogger confirmed the old man's identity. Indeed, this was the same old man who—as *The Courier Gazette* and *The Camden Herald* reported—awakes every morning at 5 a.m. sharp; cloaks himself with the tattered, grayish white shawl; takes his seat on the green park bench; and silently talks to the sea. Regional reports claim this man harvests the origins of the universe in his psyche, but reporters couldn't crack him to utter a Word. However, a keen investigative journalist might <u>figuratively drill a porthole into the old man's skull—angling for his secret with the sea.</u> The journalistic prodigy aimed to <u>separate secret from hook.</u>

Linken let me say hi to the old man first, and I told him sweetly my name was Epiphany, patted him friendlily on the back. He jolted electricuted like by thunder! Oh my!

The old man said his name was Lion. "Like the ferocious wildcat?" the more insightful of the youthful journalists inquired. "In a sense," the old man replied with a crackly voice. "Like King Leon of Sparta." Lion spoke with frailty—his crusty mouth paralyzed from neglect of use.

Lion talked like he was shy to be old & had his kisser stuffed with seaweed. I said "We love you, Lion. You are like my grandfather who made me! Tell us your secrets! Linken tells me you know the auragin of the worlds."

Lion quaveringly beckoned the aspiring writers to sit on either side of him on the green park bench. "I am struck by an epiphany," Lion spoke, louder now, revitalized after decades of stagnation. "You have saved me from my limbo, children. You have rescued me from purgatory. Now I may impart upon you my wisdom, and with it you may do as you please. I am free now. I pay no mind."

Lion's mumbles changed into clear speaking and big words…good for you Lion!

The declaration about to be made—copyrighted and patented by Lincoln S. Topper on 3/3/98—is to be the most cataclysmic, Pulitzer-deserving (or rather, "desserting") declaration in time's history. It shall shame Big Bang theorists, who'll bang their heads against the All. <u>Roll your drums and lick your tongue</u> **THE UNIVERSE IS A GIANT COOKIE.** In 1701, a fig fell on Sir Isaac Newton's head—alerting him to this fact, which Newton christened "The Cookie Theory." The eve before he was to publish his discovery, Newton died—but not before whispering the theory to a child prince from Greece. The prince passed the theory down generations with a pledge to keep it in a jar.

What a fun, fruitfilled day! Lion taught us that Planets are sweet cookie chips baked with sweet fruity figs. Some chips are rocky and hard to bite on, some are soft like marshmellows and you can flatten them with your tongue! Yummy!

With the rare genetic exception, the human mind is physiologically incapable of comprehending the concept of timelessness. There was no beginning to time, and time will never end. Yet a few scholars—from Newton to a mere handful of brilliant journalism students—indeed grasp timelessness, and thus comprehend **The Cookie Continuum**. This article attempts to describe, and even sample, the origins of the universe. Albeit in layman's terms for the average reader—or amateur "journalist" who hasn't a clue she bears auditory witness to an earthshattering explanation of existence. (Naturally, this may work to the young male writer's advantage as he trumpets Newton's revelation to the public.)

So, life never started because it never began, but when it did not "not not" start, life was stuck in an oven getting hotter and hotter. The gas oven is Existence. The gas got so hot, Existence couldn't take it anymore. A timer rang and that was the first sound ever in the history of no time. The Oven door popped open with a Ding and out sprang brazillions of planets baked with Goodness.

The brilliant young journalist was beside himself in exultation. But he kept calm as any good journalist would do in a war; in a science lab on the brink of a breakthrough; in a press room with the president; or at the final round of the National Spelling Bee. By contrast, his giddy co-reporter did not keep cool, but absurdly hoisted Lion to a standing stature; raised the old man's arms up and out; and danced—could it be a polka?—in the sand. Lion's stooped body stiffly swayed in slow motion. Lion's clay cheeks and jaw cracked when he smiled. He stopped, beamed, and reclaimed the green park bench in lotus.

When Lion danced with me, I wispered in his ear "tell us more how the universe was maked." He stammered "okay, but only because you danced with me." I didn't want to hurt Linkens feelings so I told him Lion couldn't wait to tell us the rest! I told Linken we couldn't hold Lion back even if he had a Maine to pull.

In an effort to bring sanity back to the milieu, Lion expanded on **The Cookie Continuum**. "The Cookie is expanding," he expounded. Every millisecond that doesn't exist, the oven (i.e., existence) is getting hotter. The oven keeps dinging, spewing out new chips (i.e., planets). The residue from the oven—a mechanism continually used but never cleaned—is forming clumps of dough in which the chips are collected and amassed. Lion explained the constellations: "Shooting stars are made out of sugar beads, and constellations comprise the shooting sugar. The dough, chips, sugar and heat form a giant cookie. The cookie is the cohesive collection of material extraterrestrial components: i.e., **the universe**. Above all: <u>The cutter does not exist</u>. *Without the cookie, there is no universe.*

It's neat that we are parts of dough because life is sweet! Treats taste nummy so we're part of a whole. (Not a donut hole ❀) It is funny that the laws of the universe alline with pie, which is a decimal that never ends and never repeats and is equal to 3.14159 measuring the ratio to the cookie's circumfrence to its diameeter. Plus pie is sweet like a cookie!

"How can you *prove* the universe originated from a cookie? Where is the material evidence?" the brave young journalist challenged. Lion unswaddled his shawl, and withdrew a locket strung around his neck. He popped open the locket and removed a thimble-sized mold of dough. He offered it to the journalists. Each partook in a tiny taste. Fig.

The universe tastes like sweet seeds. The seeds make life. The life makes people. The people make dough. The oven makes planets. And The cookie is our creator:

<u>*There's no Wrinkle in Time.*</u>
<u>*It's Ironry, because The Timer is Always Ringing,*</u>
<u>*but there is No Time for us To Count.*</u>

Lion spoke one last time that didn't exist: "Listen closely, sage students," he said. "I've imparted upon your buds the origins of the universe. **Follow my instruction and you'll go far: Embrace your egghead, and always walk a fine line.**"

MY epiphany at that precise moment: <u>I will write my life away to be a egghead!</u> Life is not straightforward, but <u>a swirl of words that make wonderful lines</u>. Thank you, Lion.

Lion bowed his head and bid adieu to the aspiring young journalists. He bloomed a little on the green park bench that morning, and resumed his silent conversation with the sea. The train trip back to Chicago was productive for the male journalist on the cusp of scientific stardom. The journalist pondered the revelation; exerted exhaustive mental energy to grasp the physics and calculations behind **The Cookie Continuum**; succeeded!; and triumphantly wrote a press release touting the breakthrough. The brilliant journalist compiled a mammoth media list.

My flight home was very peaceful. I like Maine.

Now home, the fame-destined journalist has notified—by telegram—the news to the newspapers, Ivy League universities, and TV stations across the globe. At this very moment, the telegram is being read by the most astute, influential figures in Science and Media. Due to self-forecasted demand, the brilliant journalist will not remain enrolled in this Journalism Class, but nonetheless, expects a cordial A on this paper. Oh, the journalist's phone is ringing now. Excuse him, he has to get this.

This was fun! Writing is happyness! Makes me hungry for fig newtins (☺)! I'm going to eat them watching TV. After all this thinking, I think I deserve some rest & me time! Mom left cnn on, something breaking news it looks like, but I'm switching to Friends.

The Universe

Sarah Charles
Creative Writing
Professor Schaefer

I Will Not Let My Willow Weep

My Nana's painting is maybe 200 years old. Nana's Nana bought it for her (my Nana) from a street vendor at an outdoor art fair in Savannah along the walkway canal. Nana said even back then were there cobblestones or bricks or something solid her little feet could press down on so that she wouldn't sink.

Nana was wearing pink or yellow, a bonnet maybe, ruffles with a dress. She didn't exactly tell me this, but I see her when I play her old movies in my ivory-tower theater upstairs. That's where I run the film and watch in the wings. There is colour in the past during the parts where I close my eyes.

My Nana's wings budded and bloomed when I turned 20. She burst up to the heavens like a love sick woman holding her heart, yearning in breathlessness uncapturable. Now Nana's an angel. She took her stories everlasting to the heavens, but laid a few still here to linger for a lifetime or two.

She was a beautiful girl. Cherished like be all children should. She wanted that painting with so much yen her Nana paid the vendor for the watercolour, gifting it happily to make her granddaughter. This gave her (my Mama's Mama's Mama's Mama) heart a warm stir.

Now the little rectangular painting hangs snug and cozy on my little book room, "the library," wall. In my little gingerbread house home. It dons a pointy roof, shingles, trim and shutters, and an ornamental chimney that doth lead not to a fireplace. It's a home perfect for one like me and a tree.

Cherished like be all children should

My painting lived a short time with my own Mama. She hung it caringly in the family kitchen. My Mama's still on the vale of stage or afterwards maybe it's the theatre comes. When I my gingerbread house bought, with the pennies from my change purse, she gave me Nana's painting as a christening. That was Mama's turn to stir her heart warm.

My painting is a milky lilting watercolour. A willow tree with a royal blue trunk I hug with my soft still arms. Branches dangle soft greens and pastel blues. It drinks from a tiny pond or oasis at its base through its winding roots that entwine into my walls hunkering, tucking itself in. Only thorns at its wrists for grip.

It's my willow now, and I've nurtured her since childhoods. It is rimmed in grains of sand or maybe the artist ancient made it in the liking of a burnished shore. My willow will live in my love and linger. For a lifetime or two. If not here with daughters and sons, then up in the rows. A home willt it always be handed. I will never let my willow weep.

Assignment: How will you apply your college studies to your future?

Hilly-Rae Lime
Teachher Schaeperd
Comp 1010

My pHd is fur the Sabbathical, not the Celery

Intrestingly, I will apply my **CURRANT** college nowledge to my **FUTURE** college nowledge, but on a smarder level.

After I get my assosheiates degree I'll get my pHd. If CLC offerred pHd's I get mine here. But I asked at reception and she told me no. She said I "need a batchler furst"—but I must fined **MY SELF** befour I fined a husbend. Then she said some thing like "your master" but when I **DO** fined my husbend, I'm not gonna let him tweet me like that.

Hmmm, I wonder **WARE** to get my pHd. May be I apply to northWesturn, so I'd get alott of money like the northWesturn students got. Or may be I apply to that **OTHER CLC** branched in Vermin Hills. Then I'd not **HAVE** to transfur, Ida only have to change schools.

I dont want my pHd to think bedder or fur the high celery. I want my pHd fur the Sabbathical. Tiffani with Trinity told me pHd students take Sabbathicals. MOst Sabbathicals last 1 year, but some last 10 years and I want mine will go to 11.

I am a spiritual person: it's in my biowlagee. I was born with a pendant fur helping peeple. That kind of self depprickdtheyshun is like Jesus depikted, and is also biowlagical. Jesus was a man like all of us. He still **IS** a man, but he lives **INSIDE** us not in his body like a man does. I'm not even a man but I feel like one becussz Jesus lives inside me.

Thadt's why I choose english be my pHd majer. To spread the **WORD**.

When I herd about Sabbathicals from Trinidy with Tiffany, I new God was speaking to me Hilly. His voice was shiney wet and warm like a waterslide of sun beems. If evrey pHd gets a Sabbathical, that means all pHds are religioused like me. (Accept pHds who jusdt wants to get payed to take a free vacashon. THAT'S a sin- almost as bad as Sucklarism like at librarys and post offfices)

If I take my Sabbathical at Lourdes in Swizzerland, I will CLENSE the cripples. I will not Basque in wholly waders. And even tho its legal in southern Urup, I would keep my bottoms on. Peeple without pHds are not very smard, and many are not Christen beliefers witch means they are not very smard. They probly dont even NO what Sabbathicals ARE.

I no: Sabbathicals are when you spread the Word of God by traveling far a way to a faraway county, a way somewhere far. There you meet village sinners or idiot village childs of sinners who are not smard enuff to see the light EVEN THO God's light pennytrades us every DAY.

It's a pHd's MISSHEN to teach villagers that to get to Eardth, we have to see Heavan furst.

"Once I saw a peak of heavan on my preschool's freshly moad football feeled by the bleechers.

I was alone with no body but my owned. I was resting happyily on my back like a snow angle in the tall hot grass.

Peering up at the clowns fluffy ruffels a flash of white lite churned into a bitty bubbel that floated down to me. I saw a little man with white beerd inside the bubbel. He wore crooked glasses and carreed a shephard's staff.

It was our shephard of heavan! I looked closer and saw his stafff was a PEN.

Don't pop our Afterland misster shephard!!! The bubbel blew a way."

I will choose where I will go to live. Brazills need Sabbathical takers. I dont understanded this becussz Brazills has a big statue of Jesus on top of a big hill overlooking the city and is where ardists Pickasso, Van Goed, Moneighed, and Caboose LaTrack painted. So Brazill dont NEED guidants becusz ardists are already lost seuls.

No, I thindk my Sabbathical better be better in Congo, Russha or Chilly. I can spred the Word in Congo good thru repercussions with marahkas. An I can spred the Word good in Russha becauzs I move fast around. And I can spred the Word good in Chilly becussz I've 2 harts to warm people: Mine and Jesuses. Or may be I'll teach english in Sangria sence Sangreans speek spanish.

Peeple I will meat by going door to door or tent to tent if they dont have doors. Or tree to tree if they dont have tents or air knock if it's a dessert. I will tell them how LOVE is the best medicine when you dont have any and even when you do, its still the best medicine becuzsz its free excepdt in amsterndam. I'll invite the villagerrs to my bungalowed to heer me reed storyes. They wont understand english but they will understand the langwidge of the Lord.

Amen to get all A's. My future so brite I have to prayer grades!!! !
When I accept my deeplahoma I will stand up to Northwestum or Vermin students and speek into the mikerfone:

Free at Lasdt! Free at Lasdt! Thanks the Word All Mitety I'm Free at Lasdt!

Sam Serriff
Visionary &
Aspiring Intern
Professor Schaefer

The Intrinsic Quandary of Unionizing Interns

Students consider college unions a space to study, listen to live music or poetry readings, fraternize with fellows, play pool or Pac Man, and have a beer on the terrace. All while watching the sun set over whatever college town it is.

To a scholastic few, I myself included, college unions are a forceful structure. They are symbols of progress. They are vital to the academic commonwealth. There are unions for the tenured. There are unions for the adjunct. There are unions for the emeriti. Yet, there is a glaring gap.

It's common practice an intern is overlooked or, more vulgarly, "looked over." It's socially engrained in our psyches. Think "Intern." I bet you're envisioning coffee fetcher, gypsy in a pencil skirt, meek apprentice, or at its worst, hussy.

No, Internship is not descendent to the oldest profession. By their own ambitious design, interns are the conduit from teacher-to-student, the midwife for enlightenment's offspring, the circulatory system that helps the heart pump intellect throughout the student body.

I argue that interns are courageous warriors, willingly putting themselves on the front line. They expose themselves to judgment and ridicule. Yet their reward on payroll is pocket change. Clearly, interns are a visionary crew. So why is such a brave band so disjointed?

To answer this question, we must consider the troops' composition. Interns are a certain breed, typically well bred. I, myself, aspire to be an intern of English Composition at this fine facility, or, perhaps Champaign Urbana. I *choose* to challenge mockery to a stare-down. Will I stare by my lonesome? This is a call to unify!

Interns have a *right* to fair pay. Interns have a *right* to school-paid healthcare. Interns have a *right* to call the shots. Interns have a *right* to challenge their mentor in class. And, yes, interns have a *right* to pensions.

I'm not the first to demand intern unionization. In June 1964 *Wanda A. Roundalott* of Mississippi Delta Community College rallied 2 English and 1 Fine Arts interns to march at the Moorhead Chamber of Commerce. (Paid $1 an hour, *Roundalott* had been dismissed for demanding 10¢ an advance.) *Roundalott* championed the march, but townsfolk were unfazed. Their attention was compromised by a riverside concert by *Johnny Russell* (country music legend and Moorhead native).

5 years later at Iowa-Tech (now Indian Hills Community College), *Porta Poitier* ignited an energy to unionize interns in Humanities. She and her league of 2 fanned smoke signals–spelling "Interns Unite" in the sky. Tragically, a charge of arson singed the girls' hopes of ever teaching again.

A more recent attempt was in 1983 at Mid-Plains College–the oldest community college in Nebraska. *E.T. Elliott*, a bright intern in the Poetry section, was outraged. To his surprise, he discovered his activities consisted of stapling handouts and massaging the professor's weary feet after standing lectures. *Elliott* took to D.C. and pitched camp on the White House lawn. One drizzly afternoon, *Elliott* held high a sign that read: "Unions for Interns." (While he did not realize his dream, he did realize the ink on the "U" ran to form into what looked like an "O," which explains why he went home crying.)

I, *Samuel Serriff*, will follow *Roundalott*, *Poitier*, and *Elliott*! Times have changed: Interns are stronger than ever–dodging between bodies like agile waiters at trendy Manhattan restaurants. But, there is 1 dilemma. The elephant in the room...

Turnover.

Interns in academia tend to last one semester. Evidently, they do not feel valued as educators. Although, ironically, the majority move forward to become just that! Take that, skeptics!

It's no wonder interns flee their posts. They suffer smirks from students and teachers alike! Well, I call on all teaching interns in America to sit at *my* lunch table. We will *demand* our entitlements with force! Interns in all departments–English, Science, History, Math--will multiply! We will *mobilize* and found the "Unionized Multiple-intern Movement" (UMM).

We'll *stay put* in our posts. We <u>will</u> <u>not</u> move on to job security, higher pay, respect, and stimulating academic assignments; *because,* as unionized interns, <u>we</u> <u>will</u> <u>already</u> <u>have</u> <u>it</u>.

HELEN STAMFORD, PH.D.
AUDITING POETRY, MY ENRICHMENT
T. SCHAEFER, FELLOW FACULTY

ON AURAGIN OF THESES

AS PROFESS<u>OR</u> OF <u>A</u> <u>DOCTORAL</u> **PROGRAM**
I<u>LL</u>-ADVI<u>SING</u> A <u>STUDIOUS</u> **CLAN**
I CON<u>FESS</u> MY <u>PROGRAM</u> IS <u>A</u> **SHAM**
IT'S FOR <u>FEAR</u> THAT I <u>WILL</u> GET **CANNED**

<u>ALL</u> OF MY <u>STUDENTS</u> ARE **BRILLIANT**
GREAT <u>MINDS</u> LIKE AT <u>PRINCETON</u> OR **YALE**
THEY <u>RIGHTFULLY</u> <u>CLAIM</u> THEY'RE **RESILIENT**
SO I'VE NO <u>CHOICE</u> BUT TO <u>MAKE</u> THEM **FAIL**

I <u>MENTOR</u> THEM ON <u>THEIR</u> **DISSERTATIONS**
YET <u>DIPLOMAS</u> FROM <u>THEM</u> I **ROB**
WHY <u>SHOULD</u> I GRANT <u>THEM</u> **GRADUATION**
WHEN <u>ALL</u> THEY <u>REALLY</u> <u>WANT</u> IS MY **JOB**

IF <u>THEY</u> <u>GRADUATE</u> I AM **HISTORY**
SAME <u>CREDENTIALS</u>, SAME <u>PRESTIGE</u>, PLUS **YOUTH**
WHAT WOULD <u>HAPPEN</u> TO <u>ME</u> IS A **MYSTERY**
I'D SUC<u>CUMB</u> TO <u>GIN</u> AND **VERMOUTH**

<u>SOME</u> FIND HEXES **SUPERSTITIOUS**
BUT <u>I</u> CAST A <u>LASTING</u> BAD **AURA**
THE <u>TRUTH</u> IS I'M <u>VEXING</u> AND **VICIOUS**
I'M THE <u>FAUNA</u>, MY <u>STUDENTS</u> THE **FLORA**

<u>SECURITY</u> OF <u>TENURE</u>'S A **FABLE**
LIKE THE <u>RUMOR</u> MAN <u>WALKED</u> ON THE **MOON**
WHY SHOULD <u>I</u> THESE YOUNG <u>EINSTEINS</u> **ENABLE**
WHEN THEY'LL <u>SANDBAG</u> ME <u>WITH</u> THEIR **LAMPOON**

IT'S <u>NOT</u> LIKE I <u>DEEM</u> I'M A **WASHOUT**
I'VE GOT <u>SPINE</u>; I'VE GOT <u>CLOUT</u>; I'VE GOT **CLASS**
<u>UNIVERSAL</u> <u>WISDOM</u>'S WHAT <u>I</u> **SPOUT**
<u>THEORIES</u> I PULL <u>OUT</u> OF MY **MASS**

WHEN AN <u>ESPECIALLY</u> UNNERVING **VIRTUOSO**
SASSY, SMART, <u>STUCK</u>-UP AND **SNIDE**
CHALLENGES THE "<u>F</u>" GRADE I **BESTOW**
I FAKE SOUR<u>CES</u> AND DECLARE <u>IT</u> **PLAGIARIZED**

THE <u>DEAN</u> HAS NOT <u>YET</u> RAISED AN **EYEBROW**
THAT <u>NONE</u> OF MY <u>STUDENTS</u> GET **THROUGH**
SO <u>LONG</u> AS I <u>CONTINUE</u> TO **KOWTOW**
HE DOESN'T <u>CARE</u> TO <u>CRITIQUE</u> MY **REVUE**

I DON'T <u>PITY</u> MY <u>PROTÉGÉS</u> THOUGH EACH <u>WORKS</u> **HARD**
LIKE AN <u>APT</u> AND AN <u>ABLE</u> **APPRENTICE**
IF THEY <u>MUST</u> PRINT "<u>DOCTOR</u>" ON THEIR <u>BUSINESS</u> **CARD**
THEY CAN PUR<u>SUE</u> A CAREER AS A **DENTIST**

IF I COULD <u>TRAVEL</u> BACK <u>IN</u> **TIME**
TO THE <u>DAWN</u> OF THESE <u>DAMNED</u>, CURSED **THESES**
I'D CUT THE <u>BINDINGS</u> LIKE <u>CORDS</u> OF A <u>BOOK</u>'S **SPINE**
LET <u>MONKEYS</u> THROW <u>AT</u> THEM THEIR **FECES**

PARA<u>NOIA</u> OF <u>SUCCESSION</u>'S MY **OBSESSION**
SO <u>NATURALLY</u> I GIVE <u>STUDENTS</u> BAD **DIRECTION**
I <u>COVET</u> AND <u>KEEP</u> MY **PROFESSION**
BY <u>MEANS</u> OF UN<u>NATURAL</u> **SELECTION**.

Student: Cherry Black
Class: Intro to Playrighting
Teacher: Ted Schaeffer

Hall Bell Has Broken Loose! Has Anybody Seen Alfredo? Or:
The Alarming Tale of a Missing Exchange Student…

CAST (in order of appearance)

Act 1:
Narrator
Professor Potbelly
Wilma
Velma
Gwen and Jill

Act 2:
Dean Dean Dean
Lunchlady
Janitor Jake
Harmonia
Peter

Setting: Bara College
Act 1: The Halls
Act 2: The Cafeteria
Genre: Drama, Intrigue
Special Affects: Sammy Black
Playright: Cherry Black

Act 1:

Narrator *[sitting on stool]:* The winter quarter began like all other quarters at Bara College. Bells rang tinny as foil. Student's stomped in snow. Heart's pumped hot blood down raw, boiled veins.

[Enter professor potbelly and Wilma stage left]

Potbelly: Wilma, you are a student. You have Alfredo Garbanzo in your restaurant meat cutting class.

Wilma: yes, professor potbelly. But Alfredo hasn't been in meat cutting all quarter. And we've already one week into it! I'm starting to worry. *[Wilma faces audience and smiles furtively. The smile holds great meaning]*

Potbelly *[doesn't miss a beat]:* Why are you smiling futilely? *(Wilma shuts her mouth.)*

Wilma: I'm not smiling. I'm crying behind my teeth. *[Wilma opens her mouth again. She clutches her teeth and coughs nervusly.]*

Potbelly: Very well. You may recuse yourself, Wilma.

Wilma: Thank you, Professor. I hope you find alfredo…unarmed. *[Wilma exits stage right. She shows audience she is crossing her left two fingers.] [Enter Velma stage right. She approaches professor potbelly.]*

Velma: Professor Potbelly, I just passed Wilma Headwink in the hall and she had an enigmatic smile across her cheeks and her fingers were crossed like a cruisefix.

Potbelly: How cureous. Why would Wilma smile with an enema? I just relieved her.

Velma: I simply must talk to you. I have something to confess, and I'm scared you'll think me something awful.

Potbelly: I don't think; that's why I'm here. What is your name? And what is keeping you awake at nights?

Velma: How did you… *[She shakes her head like a Housewife whose perplexed why her tub is clogged, but decides she doesn't care.]* Anyway, I cannot find my boyfriend, Alfredo. He is tall-5'9 with Boeing black hair from Grease and Rome where he's from.

Potbelly: I am acquainted with Alfredo Garbanzo. I met him at orientation last year in Bangcock.

Velma: China? But he told me he's an Italian exchange student! He says Lake Forest, IL and Rome, IT are Step-Sister Cities. *[Takes out a locket with a half heart]* See this is his Grand-mother's. She gave it to him on a roman holiday. he gave half of the locket to me as a testimonial of our love. *[She tucks the locket back in her pocket]*

Potbelly: Now, what did you want to confess, Velma?

Velma: *[hesitates hesitantly]* I feel aweful. I was cheating on Alfredo, you see, my lover and I were in shop, and I lost the locket. It has a half heart on it. Alfredo has the other half. Now I can't find him or the locket. Do you think he knows? It's not locket science. It would hurt him so. You see, his grandmother gave it to him on holiday.

Potbelly: Rest assured; I shalln't tell a soul.

Velma: You are so amicable, Professor. Sometime's I feel my head is'nt screwed on straight.

Potbelly: my dear, I may be amiable, but I'm certainly not amicable. Now go you off with your head straight.

[Velma kisses Professor Potbelly's cheek, and, clearly a wait off her shoulders, she exits stage left.]
[Enter Gwen and Jill, hand in hand in hand with fear. They are shaken like frizzy martinis.]

Potbelly: Girls, what on earth is the matter? Why on earth do you shake sew?

Gwen and Jill: *[unilaterally]* there's something queer at the college! It's pandemonium in the cafeteria! **Hall Bell has broken loose!** there's a strange thumping under floor board- people think it's a fantum.

Potbelly: The Board you say...

Jill: We have to go! Time for Federal Forensics 102 in the lab. Campus mysterys are out of our juristicktion.

Gwen: Yeah, we only do foreign assignments. *[Jill slaps Gwen in the face. Gwen mouths words "sorry" and they exit stage right.]*

Potbelly: Ah so, I must ascend downstairs to the lunchroom. [Pause- hear a pin drop] Someone has opened Pandora's lunchbox. I suspect alfredo has been found. [Stage lights go black.] [Curtain falls]

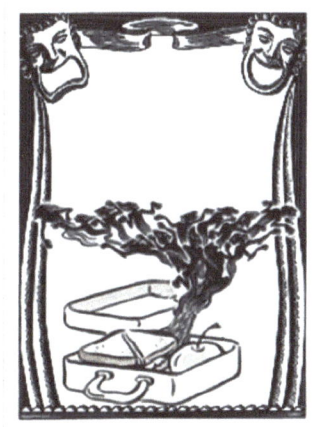

Act 2:

Narrator: *[still on stool, but at the top of a spiral bookcase like uncooked fusilli.]* Professor Potbelly had a stinking feeling he wasn't in famillar territory as he ascended downwards to the basement cafeteria he knew so well. *[Potbelly walks in place as if walking down invisible stairs. He pretends to wait for an elevator door to open. He steps out. Abruptly the Dean, Dean Dean Dean appears from stage center behind a column.]*

Dean Dean Dean: Potbelly! What do you think you are doing down here?! This is no place for you. This is for hungry student's. Famished for education.

Potbelly: I am not here in the interest of food. I already ate. *[Strokes his potbelly like it's a baby in utarot]* I am here to solve the mystereous disapeerance of Alfredo Garbanzo. Have you seen him?

Dean Dean Dean: I don't confiscate students...I mean congregate with students. What are you incinerating?

[Dean Dean Dean loosens coller, exits left muttering] The Board must not know. The Board must not know.

Lunchlady *[voice only]*: Hay Handsome! Put yer hands up! *[Potbelly jerks around and puts his hands up. The voice is coming from the audience. Potbelly puts his hands up.]*

Potbelly: I didn't mean to...I mean, why are my hands up? Where and who are you? *[The Lunchlady is sitting in the front row and she stands up and turns to the audience. She yielding a meat cleaver.]*

Lunchlady: Don't you see? Can't you see his guilt clogging his face? Here, let me drain it for you. Oh Potbelly had a lunch box alrite, filled with pasta alfredo, and he ate every last bite except the arm....ahhh! *[A bang sounds. Lunchlady falls to the floor and remains there until the ovation.]*

Potbelly *[to hisself]*: That's preponderous! What would I do with armor? I say, who shot the Lunchlady?

[Janitor Jack walks down a row through the audience with a mop whissling. He steps up on stage and faces Potbelly. He cocks his mop handle which turns out to be a sawed off shotgun before it's sawed.]

Jack: Meals over, Pothole. You're confessing or I'll roll you in plastic and drag you to the can. *[Moves ashtray aside to points to recycling bin.]* Alfredo used to nod at me. And you made him disappear. I'm a man too! *[Potbelly is about to scram when there is a scream as Harmonia enters stage fright]*

Harmonia: There's thumping under the floor board! Something's alive down there! Peter, help me! *[Harmonia's boyfriend Peter runs in stage right too and sweeps her off her feet. He has on no shirt on <u>but he is wearing a locket with half a heart.</u>]*

Peter: I left shop when I heard you screaming. I'm hear baby. I'm so relieved you're screaming about the board and not my missing shirt!

[Special Affect: Under stage where there is a trap door the floor boards move up and down and there is a loud thumping that sounds like a heart boiling with fury and raw with heartbreak. A mysterious buzzing.]

Jack: Speaking of missing… *[he opens up the floor board and a lone arm flails out, thumping on the stage floor. Jittering. An electric blanket covers the actor so the audience does not see the rest of his body or head under the trap door.]*

Wilma and Velma: *[Wilma enters as Velma enters stage right.]In unicef]* Alfredo! *[They look at each other startled.]*

Velma: Wilma. **Wilma:** Velma.

Harmonia: Oh my God. Alfredo has no body! It appears its been eaten. But He's holding something in his arm!

Jack: *[approaches the skittery arm whissling.* He pulls from its clasp a locket with a half heart *and holds it up for the audience to see shiney before returning it to the arm's hand's grasp.]* It seems he had a love. *[Looks at Peter's locket. Harmonia flinches. Velma looks away.]* Judging by the snarky bites by his shoulder I'd say he was eaten.

Wilma: Does this mean Alfredo's exspelled? He was going to help me with this tick with my fingers crossing and my smiles stretching creepy. Phooey. *[Exits dishmayed]*

Velma *[walks up to arm]* Oh alfredo, how could you do this to me. *[She looks at Peter and then back at the arm.]* You should have told me. I would have understood. You're European. *[exits wheeping.]*

Peter *[turning to Harmonia]* This is inane! How did he get my heart? Velma gave me this! *[Harmonia is stunned.]*

Peter: Uh…to me…to give to you. *[He unclasps the locket and puts it around Harmonia's neck. He whips the precipitation off his forehead with his palm when she smiles sweetly, believing him.]*

Harmonia: Oh, Peter. It's lovely. Why don't you show me that shop room you're always keen to go on about. Show me where you keep your screw drivers and nails! *[Peter perks up.]* I'd like to build you a little birdhouse for your garden with a little door. *[Peter looks disappointed and they exit, arm in fist.]*

[It's just Professor Potbelly and janitor jack on stage. Jack whissles tauntingly.]

Jack: You lucky devil. I saw you, you know. It was night. I was watching. Was it for the sauce? Had a taste for cream?

Potbelly: It could have bean anybody*! [Looks at Jack, sighs]* It wasn't for the sauce…it was for the salad. *Those beans go so darn well with cottage. [Potbelly and jack freeze]*

Narrator: And so that's how the story ends. Professor Potbelly, about 90 pounds heavier is deemed and sworn in a reputable Chairman of the Board of Education. He beat Dean Dean Dean for the chairman ship by a unanimate vote. Janitor Jack keeps Potbelly's secret, and in return, is promoted to night watchman. *[Narrator stoops down next to Alfredo's arm.* Takes the locket from Alfredo's grip*, slips it in his pocket, shakes alfredo's hand from his dislocated arm cordially. Narrator stands up, turns around, exits whissling.*

Stage lights black. Curtain falls.]

Mary Maladies
Composition 100
Instructor: Shafre, Ted Wind

Astroprojection in the Classroom:
A Credit-Wurthy Feet

Like Bedelia Airheart, I walk on air and pixilate myself into a million cells like the cloudes she painted on Kansas or Georgia. **Amid the cluster of dinging belles and the clomping of stomping feet** between classes, I lift billowy chin and downy arms above imagination to take wings.

Ever cents kindergarland, I glide above desks, fish tanks, and snowflake doilies sticking to winter schoolhouse windows like frosty breath. Children glazed up at me as I grazed their freckled cheeks and spreckled dandelion-druffed hair. **Cascading airbourne between perky smooth bodies.** I am silk.

I'd filter thru the ceiling to escape a spelling b or peek in on Mr. Seymour's class on the 2nd floor. Once I frittered half the day away up there til naptime. **I trickled back down** because 1st gradders don't nap any. Projection is fatiguing in a restful kind of way.

Now, 13 years later, Awake and Aglow **I coast and dart across our college campus...a corn maze** of a million invisible columns. My bone chilling flights no longer for mere bemusement.

I project with honors... Alask, **my masterpiece** ungraded.

I see how you see me as collapsed flesh over my desk. My limp flesh a drowned seal, **my head a heavy cobble,** my eyes a bleary smear. Banging my brow on my desk up and down, up and down, harder, still harder, until I gain traction and push my spirit up, up and out my carcass.

Once aflight, I count the credit-barren student heads like audits, snapping snapshots of the **spoken tongue on page.** More like me roam these halls: bloodsisters, claraboyants, and Marshmallow flame blowers. Another astroprojecter, Jessie, I passed thru in the ladies. Jessie's pyrokinetic: he starts fires in Creative Friction by **mentally rubbing 2 pencils together.**

Jessie and I **play catch with our echoes,** and fly fish in Dissection, reeling in maimed frog ghosts. It's purely recreational although Jessie's invisible lips once brushed my mute throat.

I pass my 50 minutes in Comp 100 conferencing into your skull. **laden with lush pimp rose and bush.** The thrush and residual that reside within your craniem are a marvel. Your voice may be horse, but at least your head is human.

My, your brain. How your **verbs slide down its slippery stem.** How they reverberate! Oh, **to place my ethereal cerebellum beside your corporeal head.**

This, is my bone I picked for you:

My projection deserves credit. My essays may be **blank,** but I exert mental energy in my feet.

Your syllabist states we can write statements for extra credit.

Astroprojection may not be a statement, but it is *a state of mentality.* **It's a matter of grace** I be awarded an A for my gift. Cometh forth, Instructor Wind.

Award Me.

Morris Cold (student & media contact)
News writing
Prof. Schaeffer

For immediate release

Java Script: An alarming report on the direty for coasters in computer labs

Northbrook, IL

Underwriters Laboradories unleashed a statement today on the Internets, after embarking upon a new domesticated order

UL scientologists reports the utilization of coasters in community college computer labs greatly reduce risk of digital bacterial infections.

A study funded by Caribou that costed an armchair and a leg involved a reconstructed lab with 24 desktop corrugated cardboard computers

Technical engineers conducted a real simulation of scalding hot coffee— — mug and papercup— —to leave cup rings without coasters on computer tables.

The finding: Condescension from the unevaporated rings steamed screens and dampened the keyboards building sticky residue for student fingers.

UL released into the area 51 rats in the coffee-flowing lab which was contained. The rats represented the minimum capacity of students a typical college computer lab can host at safe oxygen levels

The wired rats spread interbreeding viruses across the mice using pads They were discharged at the alarm of a bell, pushed the mugs about with their noses pointedly

The pushing affixed the ring stain into the surface, releasing aromatic germs that go well with Carmel Tunnel Cinnabuns

Secondary findings include increased wrists of electric shocks.

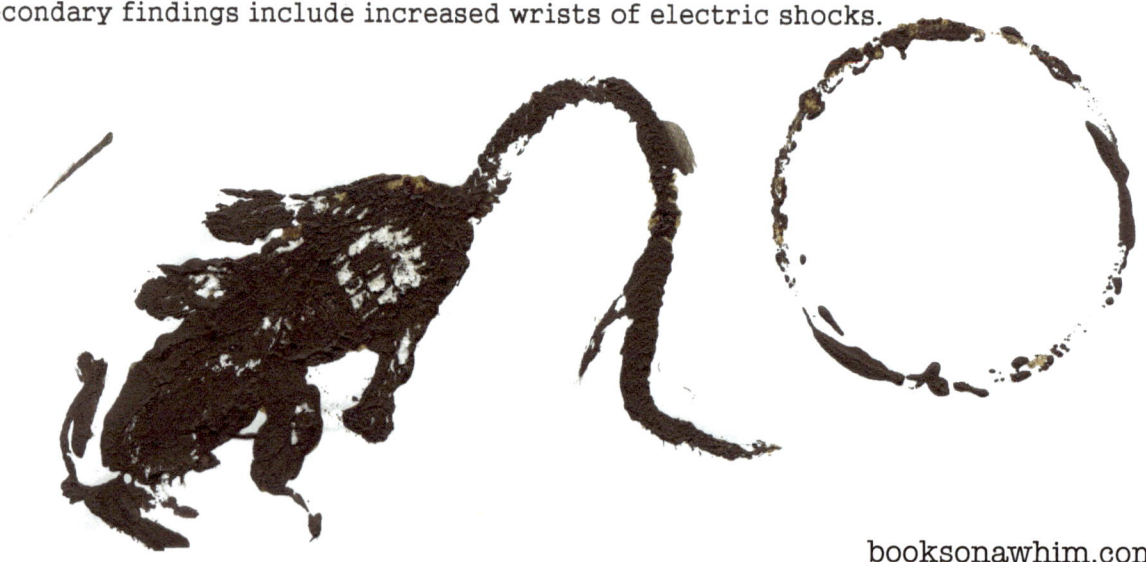

booksonawhim.com

Jeremiah Toed

Compt 1 o 1

Teacher

Teacher, please intradouche me 2 hot girl in the 1st row??.....

Wen I signed up for you're compt clast, I new that that that hottie Anita was in. Her and her fine black hare like oil thats black like oil spilling from the nuzzle.

And so long hare like Chair but more hourglass body not liked Chair but liked Penelope Crews or hot wig from Halloween stores that feels glossy in my fingerds. The stores come only at Halloween like circus's but I want them 2b opened thru all seasins like Seven11. I like 2 press buttins and make the dead bodys move and the curtined dressup room in the back of the store like nurses n cheerliters..

   Anita has shoulders she shows the class. In winter Anita wares her hot pink cashmirror sweader off her shoulder. Cashmirror reflecting lik pink shhamppain. I like Anita in sumner best than she wares inner tube topped with hip hide pokadot shorts.I never touch Anita but I peeled long lose hare from back of her sweader witch was on her body. Now her hare stranded is my bookedmark for my compt nodebook. I don't reed or rite so Im all ways on page 1 so I all ways see her strand when I lift my cover.

Since your a Teacher, u dont notice Anitas thats jail break, but you got 2 no her cus you grade her papers and she sits upfront. I here from CLC some body you have preddy wife and 2 girls to – so you can RELATE.

Relating 2 wimen is hard 4 me so please intradouche me (to Anita not your daughters.

Ways to intradouche me:

1.) Split me an Anita together as class project. Make her write dawn what I talk and make the topick be about <u>boys who was mascotchs in highschool</u> and how boys who ware costombs at baskedtball games make the best boyfrends cus they no what it feels like enclothesd. That will impress her my straynth to sumbersalt in kangeroo costumb with powch, and im shower with the Team to.

2.) Tell Anita she done stupid job writing and I done good job and thad I must have tuh give her head exercises to b bedher. Than let us in yur office n leaf us there like 3 like 4 ours. (AND turn the sign to "clothesed" hanging on your door shut so no stoodents or ur office roommate come in or wonder we don't have closed on.

3.) Give Anita a smart, precocarious stoodent's paper and fake fotocopy my name over his. Hand to Anita with an A++ like u think it's hers. Than she gets it and says: {Whose Jeremiah?!? Hes a genus at writing words So precocarious!!!!) Then u'll sweep me in with all ur mites.

3.) One day when Anita wares her cowboy booties from Pwerto Reako tell Anita thad booties are for forbiden in compt and she must go baredfeet. She prob. worried like me her feet maybe stingy, so Ill have my sisters slippers or some thongs from KMart she can slip into without beeing em bareassed.

4.) Throw a class partay and tell stoodents to bring a potluck. Tell stoodents them can bring crakers& cheez wiz, salad bowl for vegtablians or ~~fukhijnng~~ dogfood, whatever I really dont care. Bring 2 mikerowfones and carrotokey DJ whose not gay (unless hes sexie, than make him gay or id loose Anita's captivity.) DJ must play "I got u babey" by Cloudy and Chair. Anita will sing with me in tuned or out.

5.) B4 class, brake the desk table-part of the desk that Anita sits in mostly. So when class start, she puts her pepsi can on desk top and it breaks and spills. Ill be ready with mine unattacked desk top and Ill act like I brake it off 4 her like supperhero. I give it to Anita so she can keep writing and pass compt un-F'ed.

Teacher, ur the 1 who went 2 college, so you decide how 2 introdouche me to Anita. But PLEAZZ tell me which way B4 class so I come prepared.

I need to no if I have to pick up any thing up at the store. If you choosed the salad bowl (#4) I don't wanna bring the Thongs (#3). Led me no. I owe u 1,

QWERTY Keys
Comp 1

Etpgrddpt Dvjsrgrt
Professor Schaefer

You can write in your coffee table book: Pencils encouraged!

Pinocchio Malwired: The Leftover Secret Code

O', s tpnpy, mpy s dyifrmy. O siesud esmyrf yp nr s trsi npu. O vpir yp

dvjppi yp irstm jpe. O ntplr fpem isdy errl om yjr iimvj iomr. O ntomh

iu gppf yp dvjppi mpe. O', mpy yjr yuIr yp esdyr. Mpe O yuIr irgypbrtd

Omboyr ir pbrt. Og dpirpmr epiif pmiu gohitr ir piy, O'f nr tohjy pbrt.

CAN'T CRACK THE CODE?

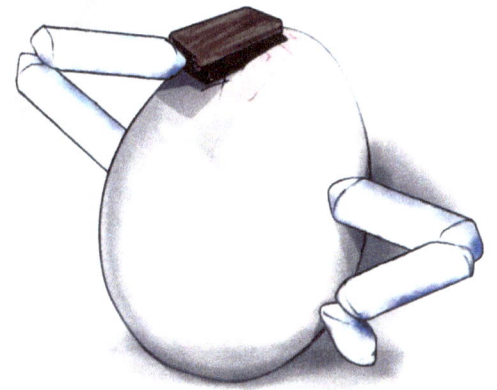

Find the translation on the
Grade A Papers Cheep Sheet

Donnie Muhwee
CLC Composition 102
Teacher Schafer

"Time Outs" Made Me A Better Man

My mom, bless her heart, was strict. As long as I knew her (& I still know her) my mom followed a doctrine she christened "Rosy Rearing". To be rosy-reared means mean kids are razed in a non-violence, anti-corporate punishment setting, like a cozy kennel for lost puppies. My mom's strictness, you see, was her *abstainment* of strictness.

My holed entire life, my mom never yelled "Donnie, pick up the pace!" or "Donnie, stitch my stocking!" like the other moms. I was allways allowed allowance without bail. I warrant ever screamed at, never had my wrist clenched by her firm fist, never slapped for stealing cokkies from the cokkie jar.

Above all, I was **NEVER** given a "time out." It didn't matter what I done. I tested her and swore. I tested her and pulled hair. But whenever I tested, I failed. My mom abode by her "Rosy Rearing" and never timed me out. Yet my happiness warrant heartfeldt. I felt a hole in my heart that I now relevate to be emptiness. What could I buy if I never paid for the error of my ways? I was a broken soon-2-B man, planted to bloom. **BUT STUCK JUST GOING THROUGH THE EMOTIONS.**

And then I met Stephanie. Stephanie has pretty thick, permed hair that cascades to her shoulders in clumps. When she shakes her blond head no, her hair comes alive like Medusas. Her squirmy strands sparkle and slime like her smile. But unlike her smile, Stephanie's frown does NOT turn upside down.

We met at Lancers downstairs at CLC. We met before that too in the parking lot, but I don't count that because her hair was rubber-banded and didn't look like her really. I'm still not sure.

But at Lancers I brushed past her at the cashed register and knocked her Nestle Quick off her food tray onto her checkered mini skirt. I thought some wisecracker pulled the fire alarm because I heard sirens and her spit in fury shouting sprayed like water from the sprinklers ceiling!!!!

Stephanie

Whoa. Wow. What a woman! I had never surveilled such **PASSION** manifester itself like that IN ONE STUDENT BODY. Stephanie shreeked me things like "Dimwit!""Nitwit!" "Dumbell!" and "Twit!"! Then our eyes met like they were crossed in the middle. This made Stephanie twinkle. She wisspered she had a secret...for me to lean closer. I leaned closer and she bit my ear. Next thing you know, we're toasting our 1-ear anniversary this semester. (We live together as wife and husband. Though we're not married, I'm waiting for Stephanie to propose me.)

"What could I buy if I never paid for the error of my ways?"

Now my rosy-reared days are in my behind. Stephanie treats me bad, and it's about time! When I forget the milk, I get TIMED OUT in the closet. When I remember the milk but get the wrong percent, I get TIMED OUT in the tub. When I remember the milk and get the right percent but drop it to splatter on the sidewalk, I get TIMED OUT. Once in an electrical circuit box somewhere I don't know because Stephanie blindfolded me and jabbed a flashlight in my back. I felt cold shocks so I think I was at a jail or secret goverment factory.

Time outs give me quiet time to think about my mistakes. Like once I was making Stephanie dinner and I sprinkled sugar on her spaggetty as a romantic jesture. Stephanie took one bite and spit it in my face! It got in my mouth when I closed it to not protest. She was right to spit. It DID taste like syrupy paste.

All hell froze over when that paste hit the fan! (That ceiling fan had been a housewarming gift from Stephanie's aunt Salle. Stephanie loved the blades, how they sparkled like razors when they spun. She Cloroxed them daily with Lyscol.

The fan was spinning, so when the blades caught wind of the sweet sticky noodles they clogged its motion—slicing the sauce into a billion tiny stars spraying across the living room, dining room, and kitchen which are inside one room because of rent.

I don't remember what happened next. My neurologist thinks I blocked it. But I DO remember something with a crate and serrand-wrap. I had gotten pretty krafty at guessing which spot I'd end up in (a closet, a tub, the garden shed, a car wash, the Pizza Hut delivery wagon). But I never had any crate expectations, so this one was a tadpole unsettling. I don't recall much, but I *do* recall feeling somehow UNDERGROUND. There was lots of wisspering and foot tapping above.

I didn't call out loud for help because naturally I must have been under a library, and because I knew Stephanie'd get me when she was good and ready. This time out in particular proved to be particularly dehydrating. But it was all part of my inside path to becoming a better man on the outside when I'd get there. A good man might protest, but a better man would endure.

When Stephanie finally arrived I was a blender of emotions: over joy, grateful, my tears slipping my squinting eyes open from the lite. She could have kept me in the crate for years *but she CHOSE to free me*. I was touched that she brought me a blanket and a bottle of water. While Stephanie may not have spoken, her eyes said "I do love you, you know Donnie." I said, "I know you do", and she looked at me funny since she hadn't said anything.

It's not like I *like* being timed out. Frankly, there are times it's downright terrifying. But usually I just get the shakes—a survival mechanicism which keeps my blood circulating. You see, I never try to escape because I want Stephanie to marry me. And it feels good to know she cares. I'm finally secure in my own broken body, in my own surroundings when I recognize them, and above all in Stephanie's arms, her tight grip holding me from harm. She doesn't want to lose me either.

"I'm finally secure in my own broken body, in my own surroundings when I recognize them."

Oh mom, if you could see me now (are we still on for lunch at the Gurnee Mills food court Tuesday?) you'd be so proud that I have crouched into my manhood. I cast you no scorn for your failed child-raising. How could you have known, being a married mother of 5, that children need discipline? Or that "Rosy-Rearing" STUNTS A CHILD, NOT GROWS THEM UP. Well, the *important* thing is we're all good now. You. And me and Stephanie.

We're all in our proper places. Some smaller than others, in fact my neck...

...is it...? I think it is... Stephanie's footsteps....yes! Time's up.

Nora Lane
Comp 1. Collage of Lake Country
Professor Schaeffer

**From Stall Secureity to the Hippo Campus:
How to Make Collage a Better Insditution**

I am really glad that you asked me to write on making collage a better insdition. I am really glad cause I have alott of ideals. **This writing asignment is really good for the future of our collage.** I am trilled you will bring our papers to you're boss's to make these changes happen. I am really excited to be at CLC when they make my changes.

Pilantrophy

I am a faithfilled beleiver in taking my morals to school. So CLC will be **burning sinuous books** in the CLC liberary. Actuary the burning is better *outside* the liberary so the good books don't get burned up like the <u>Always Freinds Club: Cricket Goes To The Dogs</u> by Susan something. The 1st book to burn is <u>A Prayer for Owen Meany</u> by John Irvy cause no buddy should prays for meanys no madder how much they own.

Book Burning

Humaniterian jesters are cridical to improve collage insditutions. CLC will lunch a **fund to save the citisens of Ice Land**. People and women and childrens are slipping all over!!! It's a really catasstrophy that we cant imagine cause we live in a 3st world county with water.

In Ice Land the school busses busses don't have 4-weel drived. So CLC will rais $ to ship Ice Land more weels at least 3 so the childrens get to school safe and eat soup that's hot but not to hot or it will melt.

Ice cube Fountaine

To rais $ CLC will scullpt a Fountaine in the faculty lowwnge that's freezer to. **The Fountaine will spray ice cubes** to cymbalize how cold hard times must MELT
to prospbrrr cause you cant splash money into ice. But you CAN chip-away-at-it penny bye penny. So teachers will make a mandatroy wish for Ice Land and skid their pennies into it for the childrens.
But the teachers cant tell or wish wont ocme true.!!!

= Oportunitees

I just don't care about freezing counties. I care about = oportunitees for the handicapted before they fall down. CLC will **booby trap the ladys bathroom** to be a better place to go.

At the handicapted stalls a trigger will trip ununabled ladys who try to use the whale stall cause theyre shellfish.

CLC will enstall a **fingerprint scanner** to to enter like how they enter subways or buy grocceries.
All student's will must registrar their fingerprints on their student ID's'.
Handicapted student's will get pupil scans to show theyre legitimate.

But booby traps are useless without military enhancements. Lasers may also be in vein.. If all else flails than armed authoritys will stationed inside the stalls. The criminalls will be **handcufted around the knees** to keep them from going or faking.

Stall Secureity

None of this applys to mens stalls cause there's only one.
And men are not at a dissed advantage like their under parts.

My New Wing!
The word on the hall is CLC has $$ for students life. We hall know that CLC

I have a PERFRECT ideal: Rais a West Wing On Willow Way! The wing will consoulidate the **heart department**: Art is meaningless so it will mergegood with cartiology and they both can both use the same sign. Heart and Art can share utensills for graphic materiuhls. Even better yep, if workers weld

Heart department with gastronomy

the west wing **wide**, we can work **gastronomy** in to the mix. Gastronomic students can share palattes with the arts and palms with the hearts!

Moving art, cartiology, and gastronomy to a new wing will free up rooms inside the main bilding for **a nursing room** for doctorates secretarys and an **interrogation room** for plagawrists.

Plagawrists detector tests

Campus Attractscions

Outdoors of the liberary lairs in the cul de-sac of air, CLC will bild **a Zoo** with hippos, sea cows, and hippoppotamuses.

The Zoo will require maintenants: It will mergewith **neurology** to have the best at hand to understand how to handle it. Ill animals and all mammals get they're brains tested if sick in the heads. If they pass they can live there.

Brains to sick to handle

booksonawhim.com

CLC will buy girraffes who's necks stretch to the 2ent floor, and screw modern-eyed escallators on the giraffe's necks. Then student's can go up and down without walking or sliding. (The girraffes will wear plastic bags on they're huhvuhs so they can stay plugged and still stand in water.)

There will be giants girraffes

A Koi Pond Coin Pond

Koi Pond

The Zoo will be so pungent and breath take-king that Willow Lake will look like goose goop.. wailing in comparison. So the CLC lobotonists who tend the Hippo Campus will release barrals of **fancy koi fishies** into the pond lake. Cause koi are nooown to flirt and CLC is family-freindly with daycared the fishies will wear berkas to cover they're frills.

There will be stuck in a sign that says <u>Coin Skipping Allowed</u>. So visitosr who want to skips stones will skips coins insteads. This will add valew to the resservoir and be liter on the fishies headsies.

Acrademics

This collage will be a better place with thoughtfull coarses like in 4-eared instidtutions. CLC needs to be sociably conschehensus. Thereforn CLC will offer these news coarses curriculli: "<u>Women's Studys: Suttle Distinksions between Escort Girl's, Gayshaw's, and Trophy Wifes Who Get There Pools Cleaned Weekdays Beetween 1 and 3</u>"; "<u>Bi Polar Studys: White Bears Go Both Ways and other Erban Folk Tales</u>"; and "<u>Indian Studys: How to Spice Up Life Without Tinned Curry.</u>".

To be sensitive to race CLC will pave a **shorter track** to make oblique runners feel less curvy, and CLC will **integrate blackboards with whiteboards** forcing them to share an eraser.
And finale,
to be sensitive to Asian Japaknees CLC will spread **wasabi as a mandatory condiment** on Lancer's Deli subs. (Or on roasted weenies if subs is a sensitive ward for either camp.)

Party Pooper Hall

Communical Gatherings

Student's deserve meccas more then the nondemonominal warship hall for religons. For i.e., aethists deserve to warship to: So CLC'll bild the **Party Pooper Hall** for commiserating celebations.

And I gather a hookah lounge for the Apathethics.

Health and Safely

Metal health is imperative to student's perorfmance. CLC hall moniters will push a couch in to the **academic advising room** on A1. Or else student's grades (PREK-PREPHD) are at steak. Student's'll lay down and make up tails about there pasts that always comes back to getting tail cause they have tail to sell I mean tell. (I'm wearing my Freudian slip to relate to the poor Icelandic womens.) Aplying Charles Charmin's **"survival of the dimmest"** theory, advisers will select the best student's to graduate and the worst to drop out and start reproducing.

Advising Couch

Fissical health is even more important then being saneitary. This is why we will enstall **treadmills in the halls** that are disguysed as **moving sidewalks**. It's to trick lazy student's who don't want to walk to class in to running. Safely's the goal when CLC puts in **revolving doors** to enter all the classrooms. This will elliminate jams and track attendence. (With no jams when OHSHA visits the doors will not stick and by counting heads they will know how many are not lost.)

Go CLC!

I'm really *excited* about these changes! I hope they brake ground this semester. Oh, I can just imagine it!!!

I see fountaines blue.....crowds that write
Bright blessed days....for those wrong or right
And I think to myshelf .....what a wonderful school.

Yolanda Docente
Fiction 3
Creative Writing
Prof Shaffer

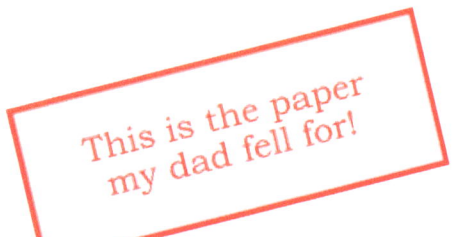

The Little Engine That Couldn't

People – in every country – know the story of the little engine that could, ahhemm, I mean, "Couldn't."

And every time they pass on there story to there children, I must intervene and say, no no, this is another kind of story altogether.

At this point the villagers gather around the fire and BEG for my story. Imagine you are now seated at the fire, in eagar anticipation for my tale: ears peeled. And now I leave you with these words, just like a waitress hands you your promised hot order, she says "enjoy." I too say "enjoy" and under my bated breath "if you can…" (Manicile laughter.)

Far in a distant woods, there were three people, two of which decided to take a stroll in the forgotten land called The Preserve. They were seeking physical wellbeing. The third, a man, was seeking intellectual well-being and decided to stay in a little coffeehouse where they served sandwiches ("enjoy"), as the others skipped and hopped through the woods in their Sunday's best.

The man entered the sandwich shop which has the façade of a train, or more specifically, of a little engine of the train. The man was delighted, as he loved trains and had a model train set as a boy in northern Minnesota. He felt inside like the waitress serving him his sandwich (no, indeed he would not wait to dine with the others) was like his great-grandmother, serving him hot biscuits and gravy on toast when he was a boy coming into the small cabin-like house after playing trains by the river. "Whoever heard of a train that could swim," his great grandmamma would claim. "What you need is a toy boat." But the man, as a boy,

This is where my dad graded this paper.
I thought it would be extremely obvious I wrote it because the bearded man character was in a train café. And…my dad (a bearded man) was grading his papers in…a train café.
My mom and I were biking on a trail while my dad graded here at The Pedal and Cup in Lake Geneva, Wisconsin.
 I told my mom about the prank when we were biking. We were looking forward to seeing my dad's reaction when we got back to the café.
But we got no reaction, because he thought the paper was genuine! (He laughed hard later.)

would always exclaim, "my little engine can." And grandmamma would retort over her tort she was baking, "your little engine can't."

The man reflected upon this as he stroked his beard and ordered his lunch. The waitress somberly presented him with a plate of toast. Normally she would flash him her shiny gold tooth, but this summer afternoon she merely clenched her teeth and squinted her eye a-gast.

"What are you doing here on earth? Haven't heard?"

"No, what's happened? And above all, more importantly, where's my gravy?"

"What a time to talk of gravey. You may as well take the gravey train out of here. There's a murdered on the lose."

The man stopped thinking of gravy, his Minnesota cabin-house, cutting the crust off his beard and stroking his bread. The waitress had gotten his intellectual anticipation.

It turns out a killer had ecsaped from the lake resort town named after an Austian Alpine village not far away, jumped off a boat on the way to an island prison and swam ashore. Apparently the killer stole a bicycle off an innocent resident's car, which had a broken bike rack and a red, white and blue bandana. Helicopters of police and media saw him bike to the very woods where the little engine sandwhich shop nestled.

The bearded man was shocked and clenched his teeth too. Oh no, my family are hiking in the woods. He clenched his teeth too and he and the waitress looked like twins. Fraternal, of course, since one was male and one was female and twins are only identical when they're the same sex.

Suddenly, ominously the waitress smiled. The man forgot his gravy and looked up. Where was her golden tooth??? Then he realized in terror…

"Waitress, if there is a killer on the lose and helicopters which I now hear above, why are you still working your shift? It can't be for the money because you are rich enough to afford a golden tooth. And I know that I overtip, but how could you have known I'd be coming?"

The waitress smiled again her Crest WHITE teeth and finished his sentence, "If I'd known you were coming I'd have baked a tort. Blood red strawberry!" (Cue manical laughter.)

The screen door banged open and a killer in a flag bandana strutted in.

"He's my boyfriend," said the waitress.

"I know, said the man," Sigh. "I know."

Suddenly an engine blew! The sandwich shop actually started to chug chug chug . It tipped to the side on its wooden track heals and started moving. The sandwich shop was really a train afterall. But who was the driver? Toast, jelly, eggs and hash flew and splattered to the walls! The waitress fell upon her outlaw boyfriend and the man took the opportunity to jump out the window just in time and in the path of his newly arrived family who were fine and confused. The three of them in silence watched the train chug away faster than a locomotive and plunge into a deep river, the deepest river in the state.

The train sank. (You can see it to this day.) The waitress and her killer boyfriend drowned, although all that was found was a wet bandana and an apron.

And yet though his life was saved and his family safe, the beared man was strangley despondent. He was thinking of the river, not unlike that of his old neighborhood in Minnesota.

"Great-grandma was right," he thought, "the little engine couldn't."

Tilly Woods Fairytails Class Professor Schaefer

I treat Bell so Well; So why is my Fairy so Mythed?

My pet fairy Bell is a beauty to be holding. She stands at maybe six inches on my palm, and when she flys away she flutters her wings and hovers over my head.

High, but low enough I can catch her. "Gotcha!" We play our game of "Gotcha!" everyday, and everynight she plays "Gotcha!" when she thinks I'm sleeping under covers.

I found Bell on a cattail sunbathing in the bog in my backyard. She had a blond pixie cut pinned up. She wore a green lilypad tied with twine. I thought she might want to play ball! So I sneaked up behind her and snatched her, and her hair turned white.

Ball didn't work out so well; Bell was clearly unclear on the concept, She thinked playing ball is running away. Fortunately for both Bell and me, fairys are slow and I'm very cunning.

I gave Bell everything fairys wish. I decorated my doll castle with white doilies, pink ribbons, strawberrys and cream Scratch N Sniff stickers she likes to scratch. I gave her my dolly's mini-dressing-mirror and wardrobe. I dressed Bell in taffyda gowns, but she got huffy.

Although she seemed to like my Glitter Barbie's visor and feathery boa. She hung the boa from my doll castle's Torch Chandelier and made a little loop like a shoe lace. Bell was making the boa into a swing! She did want to play! I surprised Bell with a Barbie Swingset, plunked her in and pushed her. I cut the boa into peaces to make a rope bridge across the bathwater moat.

I think Bell wore the Visor to hide her tears of ellation.

For many weeks Bell didn't get out of bed. She stopped flying, eating; her now dishoveled hairs' pins fell out. She slept allday. Or stared blankly at the toy TV Set with a sticker of a TV Show of a Barbie with oven mitts baking a cake.

I only catched Bell out of bed once~~flapping in my medicine cabinet opening a bottle of cough syrup. That's when I knew Bell was sick. I took out my Play First Aid kit and sticked a thermonitor in her mouth. My fairy snapped and pierced my skin with her teeth she had secretly been filing. She'd been hiding my nail file behind a poster of a sunflower in her plastic castle!

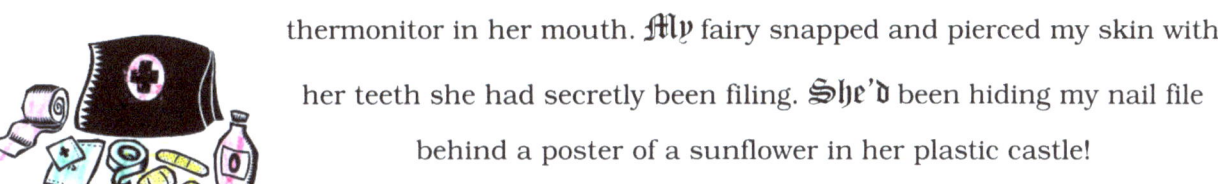

She snaps at me all the time, leering at me with green narrow eyes. Why is she so mean at me? What's there to be mythed at me for?

Now I must force her to play. When it was tea party time, I fetched my cups and saucers and set Bell up pretty with a Velcro bracelett fastening her to her little chair. Maybe I put too many teaspoonfulls of sugar in her erbell tea. When Bell kicked scalding tea on my lap with the Barbie cowboy boots I stuck her legs into, I knew an examination was needed to pinpoint her point of sweetness.

I put her in a Barbie bikini, taped her wrists and feet to the plastic bedposts. After prodding, poking and screaming, her wings were all out of order. So I freed her from the bed and taped her down to a couch and asked her to tell me her problems. She just hissed until her throat finally ran out of juice.

She's still fuming, but she doesn't hiss anymore. To think I almost kicked her outback to the mean real world. I hear fairys are like children. Someday she'll thank me.

Assignment: Write about an experience you had that involves one of the five senses

Icy Thicket
Comp 1
Professor Schaeffer

My mom wrote this paper. I'm so embarrassed.

Woo Wee! Sugars back in the limelite..! I freshened up for this moment with you, Sweets, slipped my hair back with my garter (my memento from my movie "Susie Sunbather"). Is terra cotta now-a, but in 71' was... oooh weee! ruby red like a pearl dipped in gunky cherrys. Yummy yum yummy!!

I NEW I was a writer at ♥ in 66' when I read my 1st script "Maxine Meets Maxim", I winned under-study by writing the screams in the bedroom scenes, and they got me hired.., Yippee!

Well...my pen name is DONNA and my birth name is JANET My scream I mean screen names.. oooh.... I've had ALL sorts...PATTY, LOLLY, MELONIE, CANDY, DOTS. Last Aprill, when I turned 38 again, I named myselves MOMA. Like the movie set in new york city.

(Icy doesn't call me much MOMA, but when she does, is how she frames it bristly like. Like she's a cactus without thorns that really has them. Mmmm hmmm.)

On the set of "Wild Wendy in the West" Sally 2 trailers down gives me names 2. My favoritte, tis WRITE TRASH Woo hooey! Somebody must have trolled her I'm a romance writer... Or Sally spied my nasty nice scribblilings.

When Icy trolled me she'll pay me $30 to write this paper (because she had Chest Club) on the 5 senses, I yipped, Yessmissie! Well...here we goesies!

There are billions of senses in the earth. Like...smelling coconuts and chewing leather (like in 73's' "Heidi Hides in Hawaii"). My favoritte sense, I mean Icy's favoritte, I mean, jeesh, I, Icy's favoritte sense is free love.

I met Curtis in 74' on the set of "Charlene the Cattlerancher's Calves" Curtis had just got off a stage-stint as "The Ice Man Cometh" He was still in character so we made free love in the meat freezer (I'm STILL peeling strips of ice off my back like invisible frozen strips of raw bacon.)

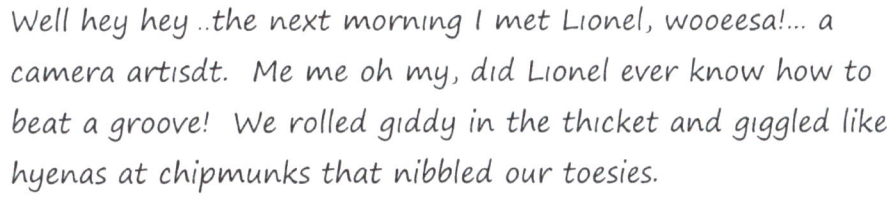

Well hey hey ..the next morning I met Lionel, wooeesa!... a camera artisdt. Me me oh my, did Lionel ever know how to beat a groove! We rolled giddy in the thicket and giggled like hyenas at chipmunks that nibbled our toesies.

Couch casting trolled me later that was the 2nd day of peek ovulation. (Just 2 days a month, men are fertile to make babies. Gee, what a cowinkedence ... Lionel and Curtis ovulating at the same window!).!

I vissoned that when Icy was born, I'd recognize her Poppy. Curtis was vanilla and Lionel was Rocky Road...all chocolate, nuts, and whip! They shared just 1 physical attribute. little feet. (All babies are born with little feet so that didn't help 1 itty bittie bit.)

All I can decider about Icy's looks is she flushes a lot. (Thow she says she just flushes when I'm along.). Since I didn't know whose Pop she sprang from, I named her "Icy" if it was Curtis and "Thicket" if it was Lionel.

<u>Maybe I made a mistake</u> with that name. like it shaped her frigid pricklly, desposition... Maybe I should'of free loved with Curtis in a damp field and Lionel in a blooming bush. Then I could of named Icy "Damp Bush", an earthy wilechild name.

Me, I'm a marvelous MOMA. Tis true!! Mornings I cook Icy breakfast.. but she never eats what I cook her! She comes in the kitchen with her threads all grey and ironed like sorrow or good taste, her hair sprayed in a bun.

Me, I'm there in kitchen... all *free* and uninhabited with my silky robe untied..... like I'm human, I'm woman that's all! Instead of saying "shine it on sister" Icy looks at me like one of them movie women who's really alien bitcsh. Not cheery like them women who give you numbers to try on clothes.

 I bellow "Icy! I made you my pancakes I'm so good at" they're my homemade batter of ground corn powder, hen eggs and cottage cheese based in cranberry sauce curdles. I EVEN serve Icy Bloody Marys o' hot sauce and vodka. She never indulges me, nope she just exits.

No **SHE** only talks to me when she wants me to DO something for her Like clean her fish tank or tell her boy callers "wrong number" when I pick up the phone sassy, or stay inside for the count of 200 when her friends pick her up.

Like this classy paper she asked me to write. Well... ok, you got me, gee golly. Okie, it's not EXACTLY the truth Icy asked me... I asked her to let me write it. Icy made me promise a A, but I'm happy living the rest of my life being B.

Jeesh Louise, you've got to understand! Ink's running through me. Pens and papers, I miss something oilful My chance o'making a splash back into the silver screen? Naw nippie, I can't fool the camera. But I CAN fool a page.

I'm only 38 I'm celebrating my writes o' passage.

I'm allowed that.
DONNA

booksonawhim.com

In-Class Writing Assignment (Comp Lab): Describe one of your greatest adventures

Ana Mona Pia
(Comp 102)
Professor Shaver

Professor, please hold me back after class! The mob in the hall is closing in on me!

Ummm...I'll start my sentence about my greatest adventure. Let's say it was...white water rafting down Nigeria Falls. Or...riding saddleless in a Spanish shark rodeo. May be...swatting flies in Nepal? Or, whatever. Ok, I think I can write now. Professor Shaver, shhh... *this is the only way I can communicate.* That is, unless my paper is bugged. (Scan for smears) There are 2 mobsters in pinstriped suits with broad shoulders out side this computer lab as I type. I'm sort of sorry for dragging you into this crime dramas, but Professor Shaver, you must help me give the men the slip. I'm trying to take off!

They have been trailing me all semester! Monitoring me like hall monitors. If I find out they're monitoring my monitor now I think I'll screen! It all started when my father, Jerry, got intelligence that I was secretly dating Mustafi. Jerry is strictly about my not mixing with foreign boys. (This baffles me since we're Sicilian) But I learnt young to <u>not</u> <u>ask</u> <u>questions</u>. Jerry said something smells fishy when he caught wind of Mustafi. That's when Jerry deployed his 2 gorillas on me. Jerry demanded I need to run with "your own kind" But Mustafi *is* kind.

When I was 4, Jerry deserted me at the spinning teacups at Kiddie Land for saying "thank you" to a cheery Mexican man behind the stand for handing me the hamburger Jerry bought me. I was on those pink teacups for *hours*. Finally, the teenager working the ride noticed me when I threw up.

All I remember about getting to our house in Indiana was the red flashing sirens in the black night during the drive and getting out of a police car in my drive way. Jerry came out on the porch and invited the 2 policemen inside the kitchen, gave them some crisp bills (probably hot) under the table. The cops left lightheartedly swinging their nightsticks with a lilt.

Then when I was 14, Jerry liquidated my 1st kiss. My 1st boyfriend Jamarkus is still traumatized (all though in his parent's case, they settled) It was only last winter when the DesPlaines River froze that the back of Jamarkus's van rose to the surface. A couple ice fishermen were pleased when they reeled in Jamarkus's weed still dry in his Incredible Hulk metal lunch box. (The lunch box was a collector's item)

Then when I was a young woman at 16, Jerry hired his business partner (Jerry runs a "dry cleaning" factory) to plant himself in the backseat of Seamus O'Reilly's station wagon on Seamus's and my's first (and last) date. It was a hot Friday summer night. We parked at the Dog in Suds to eat a hotdog and a float.

When we weren't looking, Jerry's business partner planted a stick of dynamite in Seamus's bun. Seamus's scars were purely emotional (all though his crimson hair turned white)

On the police report, the Dog in Suds blaze is coded as "accidental". The alleged cause: a cigarette butt insufficiently stubbed-out in a root beer float spiked with Vodka. The report says says the Vodka sparked the ignition. The young Russian Dog in Subs waiter on roller skates was fired. He got severance, but unfortunately for him the severance was bodily.

I know this because I dated Petrov when I was 17, before he knew who's daughter I was.

But Mustafi is different. I may be only 22 and him 23, but we are true love. Mustafi and I met in Professor Higgins's "Dialects of the World" class and ever since I'm walking in air. Studying together was so exhilarating, we classmated again in Higgins's "Creative Diction"

Mustafi has beautiful copper skin and sunkissed hair. He wraps it in a burnt orange turban. He's sweet, serene and super smart. Mustafi is double majoring in Economics and Gaming Psychology. His disertation examines (in his words) "the behavioral buying patterns of Monopoly players (ages 8+); analyzing their tabletop risk tendencies in flux with the State of the Economy over the next 5 years"

Yessiree, he's a keeper which is why I tried to keep Mustafi a secret. Sadly it was just a matter of time. 10 weeks ago, Jerry's business partner spotted Mustafi and me at The Cheesecake Factory at Orchard mall in Skokie. He snapped photos of us splitting a slice of redvelvet and playing "here comes the air plane" with our forks. The next day Jerry sicked his 2 mobsters on me.

I named the tall bony one with the long jaw bone "The Chin" and the short stubby one "The Cactus" cause The Cactus has course black prickles on his chin. (I almost named *him* The Chin) They trail me from class to class when I try to mix.

Mustafi and I created a sign language with our eyes as we cross each other in the halls. Wide eyes means "I'm scared" Eyelids halfclosed means "Pretend you don't see me" Frantic blinking means "Run" Slow motion blinking means "I love you" Sometimes we sneak seconds in solitude by the vending machine. (We buy Snickers and Wheat Thins to keep the thugs away. You see, The Chin has a peanut allergy, and The Cactus has a wheat allergy with an aversion to dieting.)

Mustafi knew what he was getting into by dating me. On our 1st date (at Lakehurst mall's Slicers's Deli) 18 months ago, I confessed Jerry's biases. I even cited Petrov, Seamus, Jamarkus and the Mexican at the amusement park. (What chance they all were all at the same mall at the same time!) But Mustafi cupped my hands in his… He said, in the proper British dialect he mastered, that "<u>Gandalf</u> <u>means</u> <u>us</u> <u>to</u> <u>be</u> <u>won</u>." (Gandalf was a bespectacled Hindu who travelled to the Middle Earth to hunt veggies.) "If that means a pre-meditational battle with your father" Mustafi said "so be it"

From the next day on, Mustafi meditated every morning before breakfast.

But it hasn't shook the gorillas off my tail! I must use militant force.

This is where you step in Professor Shaver (or Professor *Savior* if we can pull this off) At our next class (Valentine's Day) leave the door wideopen so The Chin and The Cactus can hear you. At the end of class loudly order me to stay after class. Say these words "Ana Mona, stay after class! I'm furious how close you sit next to François. How you pass perfumesented notes to Guido. How you share your chewing gumb with Santiago"

Then during your speech I will disguys myself as a guy in hooded sweatshirt and baggy jeans.

The mobsters will race inside the classroom as all students (with me in clogneato) trickle out. Mustafi will be waiting in Visitor's lot in his '81 Ford Grenada. We'll cross the countries into Jersey (The Guarding State.). It's great! Mustafi got a free pass into Rutgers new Gaming Econ Department. It's perfect, we don't have to pay tolls or anything. Plus we've got a *Get Out of Jail Free* card if things get dicey should we roll into trouble. So…

…attached to this paper is 1) my "Creative Diction" workbook 2) a pea shooter 3) A laser pointer 4) a sealed stamped envelope. Here, I have <u>your</u> directions: Study my workbook carefully. Practice aloud in the theatre wing. On the big day (February 14) bring your excellent diction to class. When The Chin and The Cactus barrel in at the bell (my escape!) switch your laser pointer on. Direct them to the wall with impeccable diction they cannot resist. Line them side by side. Press their backs against the wall, and…shoot them elocution style.

Please, Professor Shaver, do this for me.   Then just mail my stamped letter. It's to Jerry from me.

My letter says

Dear Daddy, I discovered my 2 mobsters are cousins from Africia: Ewansha and Obike. After much time together we ended up taking a liking to each other. So the 3 of us have eloped to African city Windhoek in Narnia. Love, Ana Mona.

P.S. Please give my dowry to my Mentor, Professor Shaver at CLC. I owe him my happiness. Besides I don't need dough. I have all I now need.

The Nutty Years of the Jon Stewart Presidency in a Nutshell
Featuring: The Presidents Playhouse

By Edison Bell

The Nutty Years of the Jon Stewart Presidency in a Nutshell

Table of Cornnuts

Part I
- **OBAMA RESIGNS TO HAWAII**
  - Obama Brushes off Birth Certificate
  - The First Lady Thrusts
- **A RESURRECTED ELECTION**
  - Republican Primary
  - Democratic Primary
  - The Zeppo Marx Roast
- **ART AND MONEY: CHAMPAGNE FINANCE**
  - Chicago Billionaires OutsmArt Chicago Mayor
  - Chicago Mayor OutsmArts Chicago Billionaires
- **THE DEBATES**
  - Mount Rushmore Face-Off
  - A Staged Debate
- **STEWART'S INAUGURATION AND EXECUTIVE OUTFIT**
  - The Assassination Attempt and the Spaceballs Alien
  - Colbert's Silent Tongue
  - Stewart's Cabinet Unhinged
  - Samantha's Bees and John's Olives
  - The Incorporation of Congress and the Inferiority Complex of the SEC

Part II
- **ROMANTIC ESCAPADES AND THE NSA**
  - The Sexting Scandal of Petraeus and Paula
  - E-Dating Hackers Spread Virus
- **GLOBAL FRICTION AND OTHER TALES OF DISASTER**
  - The Amazon Plant Invasion
  - An Infestation of Tics Down Under
  - McDonalds Serves Freedom Flies
  - The Study Abroad Tax Evasion Scandal
  - The Clothing of Guantanamo
  - Italy Loses Color
  - The Controversial Erection of the BOLLYWOOD Sign in Tirumala

Part III
- **DOMESTICATED NUISANCES AND A CRAZY LITTLE THING CALLED WAR**
  - Giving America the New Bird
  - Fraggles Fuss about Fracking
  - The Mississippi Missile Crisis
  - A Crockpot of Bull and the Texas Secession
  - The Perfume Wars
- **HEALTH AND EPIDEMICS**
  - The Whore on Drugs
  - The Regeneration of the Smartphone into the Human Hand
  - The Long Term Effects of Lasik Come to Light
- **AN ECONOMIC COLLAPSE AND ITS NIPPLE EFFECT**
  - The Rise and Fall of the White Bread Factory: Cutting off the Trust
  - Obama-Éclair (The Affordable Heath-Bar Act) and the Smithsonian Sweet Tooth

Part IV
- **THE PRESIDENTS PLAYHOUSE**
  - The White House is a Fun House: From Remote Control Drones to "Being John Edwards"
  - The Presidents Playhouse: A Cellar Discovery
  - Life After Laughs

Edison Bell
Composition Class
Lake Forest College
Professor Edward Schaefer

Summer 2016
Term Paper

The Nutty Years of the Jon Stewart Presidency in a Nutshell

2012-2016

Part I

OBAMA RESIGNS TO HAWAII

Obama Brushes off Birth Certificate

No American citizen or undocumented immigrant will forget the stupefying discovery of former President **Barack Obama's** *Certificate of Naissance*. Who could have guessed that forensic archeologists on a transpolar treasure hunt would unearth a flimsy rectangular document, its frozen watermark preserved. With the deployment of a protractor, ice pick and tweezers, the scientists plucked the certificate in its pristine state.

While point of conception is debatable, Obama's birth did *not* take place in the state of Hawaii. His birth took place at geodetic latitude 90° North at the North Pole, which the scientists' treasure map pinpointed as the exact location of Santa's dismantled Workshop. Obama's birth transpired long before Santa's Workshop was procured by K-Mart Corporation in the infamous acquisition of 1987 before their "Blue Light Specials" went LED.

The Obama Administration denied the authenticity of the snowy certificate. They brushed it off as some prop planted for a reality show like "The Amazing Race" or "The Apprentice." But the FBI (Federal Bureau of Insinuators) flew in a medium who substantiated that Obama, indeed, was born in Santa's Workshop. The medium affirmed, "I sense his presents." Polarized by the public, a despondent Obama withdrew from office.

However, he made a symbolic gesture in 2013 by moving to Hawaii to shoot hoops and skeet. Obama founded HULA (The Hungry Unicorns Live Association), a non-profit that raises funds and educates people on the existence and famine of unicorns.

The First Lady Thrusts

Obama's wife, former first lady **Michelle**, kept her presence public too. After the North Pole fiasco, Mrs. Obama drew awareness and crowds to her new fitness campaign: A revival of **Jane Fonda's** popular 1982 exercise videotape "Workout." Mrs. Obama introduced "Workout" to middle schools to bolster fitness and herald the historical significance of the VHS. Schools across the nation mandatorily integrated "Workout" into their gym programs.

Conservatives were majorly P.E.-ed off, and didn't take it sitting down. Their allegation: Parents have the right to opt their kids out of gym class whenever the video plays. They cited the suggestive contortions of the "Buttocks Thrust"—Fonda reclined on her back, heaving her buttocks up and down—as corruptive. Meanwhile, gym teachers (who bi-nature lean liberally) insisted their thrusts were innocent. "Students are strengthening their largest bipartisan muscle," was the gym teachers' unanimous rebuttal. "Both sides must support the other. We must not simply be fair-weather ends."

After a buddy battle, the Republicans' argument was deemed a tighter means to an end. Gym teachers admitted defeat, consoling themselves with lots of socks in sneakers.

A RESURRECTED ELECTION

Republicans did not claim victory, however, in the presidential battle of 2012—although both sides boasted formidable opponents.

On the right: **Santorum. Perry. Bachmann. Romney**. (Rumor had it **Sarah Palin** was planning to steak another slab at running, but these rumors proved ungrounded. Wary of reentering the spotlight, Palin moved to *behind-the-scenes* show business, accepting a role as **Laura Palmer's** speech coach in the 2014 revival of "Twin Peaks: Cooper Bobs for Answers.")

On the left: **Clinton. Clinton. Clooney. Stewart**. (Former Vice President **Joe Biden**, it's said, did not reflect upon a run as leading man. When Obama resigned, Biden suffered a complex stemming back to his failed Democratic Primary run for President in '88 when he was caught plagiarizing **Dr. Seuss's** *Horton Hears a Who*. So, Biden chose not to run for president in '12, disappointing himself as a running mate hopeful.)

Republican Primary

Rick Santorum only lasted one month in the primaries due to his sickening trash talk. (He caught a bronchial infection while stumping at the town dump, and admitted himself into Der Zauberberg Sanatorium in Switzerland for convalescence.)

Rick Perry did not last much longer. Perry was removed from the ballot on the grounds of his unknown geographical whereabouts. Investigators confirm, however, that Perry is alive and well and living in 4414 BC. The last time Perry was seen by modern man was March 2, 2012. He was boarding a time machine at Cape Canaveral, making a bold move to travel back in time to substantiate Creationism. Perry, the sole passenger on "Flight H.G. Well-Why-Not," evaporated with his vessel at launch.

Mrs. Anita Perry received a postcard on July 4, 2012 that read: "Hee haw! This is unf***ing-believable. It's like fireworks down here every single night with pistols, pagans, pushies, pullies, and all kinds of crazy s**t. And there are no f***ing monkeys, eat that Dems. Miss you babe, Your Perr-Bear." On the front: a photo of a Piña Colada against a sunset with "Wish you were beer!" written in cursive.

And so the Republican Primary fizzled down to a heated friendly fire between two.

Michelle Bachmann yearned to become the first Woman president. **Mitt Romney** aspired to become the first Mormon president. He lashed out that putting the "fe" before the "male" is like putting the tart before the horse. Bachmann lashed back that Mormons were Muslims that got the vowels wrong.

But Romney wouldn't have the alphabetical fuss he feared.

On May 7, 2012, Bachmann had an epiphany. She awoke at 6:00 a.m. to **Limbaugh's** light, lilting lungs on KTCN-AM. She showered; slipped into her ironed slacks; sipped her hot, freshly brewed coffee; and pressed on to read *The Telegraph* awaiting her on the kitchen counter.

The headline: "Paeleoclimatological research claims dinosaur flatulence may have warmed the earth (and extinguished the species)" (*Current Biology*, Vol. 21, Iss. 9). Bachmann spilled her scalding coffee upon her slacks. The shock of extinction by odor, she later reported, impressed upon her an awareness that it stinks life is short. "Life is a gas that can pass in a blast," she explained, simultaneously pulling out of the race and her finger. The dinosaur discovery prompted the consummation of her true calling: concert pianist in drag.

And then there was won.

Delighted by his good fortune ($250 MM) Romney took center stage in July 2012 as winner of the Republican Primary. He seemed a surefire success! That is, until the infamous controversy over his 47¢ tip at TGI Fridays (West Boca Raton). On September 17, 2012, a secretly-filmed video surfaced and went vinyl. In it, Romney brags that he tipped a Friday's waitress just 47¢ for a $10 bill. "Waitresses are not entitled to tips," he stated, continuing on to claim he has "menus full of waitresses perfectly happy to work for minimum wage alone" and "outstanding support to push the tipping infrastructure off its legs to topple." At first Romney defended his tip, but upon pressure from the Association of Waitress Elite Legion's Committee of Ordinary Meal Extravagance (AWELCOME) he later claimed he miscalculated 20%.

But the humiliation became too hot to handle after **Clint Eastwood** whispered sweet nothings to an empty chair on the stage of the Republican National Convention in Tampa, and so Romney stepped off.

Democratic Primary

It was no surprise when **Hillary Clinton** declared her candidacy for POTUS in 2008. And—despite the fact she was challenging her employer—she reentered the primary in 2012.

Republicans had no qualms about digging up a little dirt on her. They found their dirt in Clinton's '08 campaign TV commercial: "It's 3 a.m. and your children are fast asleep. But there's a phone in the White House, and it's ringing. Something's happening. Who do you want answering the phone?"

In '12 Clinton repeatedly *re*ran this same commercial. The re-airing of Clinton's ad unnerved President Obama (then still thought to be Hawaiian). He was so distressed that he went on a three-week bender at Martha's Vineyard.

After his splendor bender, a sober Obama disclosed that he had received threatening phone calls at 3 a.m. throughout his four years as president, and the eerie '08 commercial triggered his spree. This prompted a young defense contractor in Hawaii to investigate. DNA (Do Not Ask) evidence and a *Verizon Wiredlist* revealed that Hillary Clinton *herself* had been prank calling Obama. Here's how:

When Clinton was appointed Secretary of State in '09, her New Hire packet included Obama's bedroom landline # in its print directory. And so, thinking connivingly ahead to the 2012 election, Clinton routinely dialed the president from an unlisted number—exercising a variety of phonetic techniques to terrify the poor man. Her repertoire included heavy breathing; speaking in tongues; operatic warm-up scales; invitations to "play a nice game of Solitaire"; the query "have you checked the children?"; and a fine assortment of assassination threats—from slaying by spork to murder by wedgie.

Hillary Clinton withdrew from the 2012 race and switched to AT&T (which shortly thereafter was acquired by Verizon).

But there was another Clinton in the race. Hillary and **Bill's daughter Chelsea** stepped into her mother's shoes to run in her place but get somewhere. (Her mother campaigned for Chelsea, but was prohibited from making fundraising calls.) Yet Chelsea's political interests hit a yellow brick wall when she married investment banker **JP Morgan Jr.** on July 31. Now a matron with duties to look after, she left the race and moved on up to a deluxe apartment in the sky. Chelsea's philanthropic interests remained intact and she opened a soup kitchen in her $10.5 MM Manhattan condominium.

The savviest player in the '12 Democratic Primary was limousine liberal and leading ladies man **George Clooney**. He had the broads' backing and the support of the biggest names in Hollywood: From **Kevin Bacon** to **Tom Hanks** to **Leonardo DiCaprio** to **Meryl Streep** to **John Lithgow** and back to **Kevin Bacon**.

But Clooney Fever didn't last long. On Monday, August 13, 2012, an LA bouncer at *Sky Zone* (1625 W. 190th St.) disclosed Hollywood's greatest-until-then-kept-secret: Clooney was a homosexual with a penchant for male models 30 years his junior. The timing was ill; Clooney had *just* sworn heterosexuality on **Barbara Walters** one day prior to the leak. He risked penalty of perjury and going to the can! Then the damn burst to all well when DNAA (Do Not Ask Again) proved Clooney was the illegitimate child of **Cary Grant** and **Desi Arnez**. Clooney abdicated his candidacy, citing interest in "The Facts of Life: The Film," in which he would play the handyman dressed as **Mrs. Garrett**.

America was left with one man commanding: **Jon Leibowitz Stewart**.

Under Stewart's reign, Comedy Central's "The Daily Show with Jon Stewart" garnered 18 Prime-Time Emmys and a Certificate of Merit from Spike T.V.'s Guys Choice Awards for being "a generally likable guy" and "someone you'd want to hang out with."

Most Americans assume that **Stephen Colbert** was Stewart's first pick as running mate. In actuality, Stewart first approached a conflicted **Colin Powell**. Powell deliberated over Stewart's offer, but declined in order to accept a judicial spot on "American Idol."

It was then Stewart tuned in to Colbert—an equally brilliant late night comic blessed with beady, extraterrestrial eyes. The comedians knew each other well; Colbert used to serve as Stewart's squire on "The Daily Show" set and they had co-hosted the "Trash Cannes Awards" at the Oscars. (To quote former Illinois Governor **Rob Bragojevich**, the Stewart/Colbert ticket was so "f***ing golden" it could have been made by **Willy Wonka**.)

The Zeppo Marx Roast

While *almost* controversy-free, Stewart had one carry-on item of political baggage: The infamous Zeppo Marx Roast in '99. Stewart, then a fresh face on "The Daily Show," roasted his very first guest, a 98-year old **Zeppo Marx**, who was promoting his new book *Well, I Studied Comedic Dramatics at Vassar*.

Stewart, typically *commended* for his sardonic charm, verbally walloped the old actor, slamming Marx's "feeble attempts at romantic leads," "alarmingly unfunny deliveries," and pinpointing Marx's scenes as "the time when the audience ducks out of the theater to refill their popcorn buckets."

Flustered and crushed, Marx rose abruptly to leave, but tripped over his armchair—triggering uproarious laugher from the live audience who thought it part of the act. When it was later revealed the fall was NOT staged, former fans chastised Stewart, who they compared to **Michael Moore**. (In '02, Moore had distastefully interviewed a frail, disoriented **Charleston Heston** about his chew.)

Fortunately, in Zeppo Marx's case it had a happy ending. On "The Daily Show," Marx had gotten his biggest laugh ever, and by the end of the night he was beaming.

ART AND MONEY: CHAMPAGNE FINANCE

Chicago Billionaires OutsmArt Chicago Mayor

> *(Writer's Interlude: I mailed **Grade A Papers** with this version to Chicago billionaires Ken and Anne Griffin. Customizable books are a beauty of self-publishing! They didn't see Rahm Emanuel excerpt that follows or this interlude. - Beth)*

The excavation of Obama's birth certificate in the North Pole crushed moochers across America. The news was particularly gutting to Democrats in Obama's hometown, Chicago.

A lamentably "blue" city, Chicago was its bluest upon Obama's resignation. It was especially devastating for the 240,000 supporters who had gathered at Grant Park in 2008 for Obama's victory speech. Five years later, the same 240,000 crestfallen Democrats reassembled in July 2013 at the same spot during "The Taste of Chicago"—to commiserate over a hotdog and a beer. The crowd of masses arrived at Grant Park only to learn "The Taste" had moved to Wrigley Field—home to the Chicago Cubs (arch rival team to Obama's beloved White Sox).

While the self-entitled bemoaned Obama's resignation, the rich and beautiful celebrated. As the lot of Democrats wept over their imaginary beers in a vacant Grant Park, Republicans held a classy evening gala at the Chicago Art Institute's new modern wing. There was a sumptuous buffet with a pink champagne fountain centerpiece.

Chicago native and silver screen star **Vince Vaughn** served as Master of Ceremonies, unveiling new pieces of art to mark the occasion. These new pieces included **Henri Matisse's** "Sunburns by a River," **Jackson Pollock's** "Cracked Egg's Entrails," and **Man Ray's** "One Night in Bangkok Set."

The pinnacle of the party was the unveiling of two pristine life-size statues of **Ken and Anne Griffin**, the most beautiful billionaire couple *in the universe*. The Griffin statues are draped in ivory-sculpted silk sheets and ornamented with sculpted swans swimming in a marble pond at the loved ones' smooth feet. The statues—which stand hand-in-hand—grace Griffin Court on the first floor pavilion of the modern wing. (The real Griffins, also philanthropists, charitably donated $19 million in '06 to the creation of the modern wing, which explains why the Art Institute makes the perfect home for the classical statues.)

By stark contrast, the Art Institute hosts a grotesque brass statue, which was relegated to the old wing in 2013 to make room for the gala. The crooked statue is in the likeness of Chicago Mayor **Rahm Emanuel**, inarguably the nerdiest-looking Democrat in the City of Chicago. Unlike the Griffin statues—who were prudently garbed in elegant films of ivory—Emanuel was naked all but for a tiny green leaf of tin covering his groin.

Due to the drastic decrease in field trips—following Emanuel's closing of 49 Chicago public grade schools in 2013—the Emanuel statue is barely regarded.

Chicago Mayor OutsmArts Chicago Billionaires

*(Writer's Interlude: I mailed **Grade A Papers** with this version to Chicago Mayor Rahm Emanuel. Customizable books are a beauty of self-publishing. He didn't see Griffins excerpt that precedes this or this interlude. - Beth)*

Following the excavation of Obama's birth certificate in the North Pole, Chicago Mayor **Rahm Emanuel**, former White House Chief of Staff, dived back into national politics in an effort to polish the image of the Democratic Party.

Chicago Democrats—always a rowdy, optimistic bunch—rallied with Emanuel in support of a Democratically-controlled Executive Branch. The same 240,000 Obama revelers who attended the '08 victory speech at Grant Park reassembled at U.S Raise-Hellular Field in October of 2013 to "Party plan."

In a jocular huddle, the likable-minded chose to crash the Republican fundraising event "Nightie Night." (Second City class Republicans had scheduled a sassy pajama gala at the Chicago Art Institute's new modern wing. "Nightie Night" touted **Ken Griffin**, Chicago billionaire and CEO of Citadel—a portable Wisconsin gas station—who was announcing a run for president.)

The museum curator went all out with catering, which included cured salami; clébard de poisson cher (swordfish mated with lobster); an assortment of skins of Camembert, Brie and Jell-O; hairy potato-sized truffles (fungi) to be eaten with chopsticks; and cherry tomato-sized truffles (chocolate) to be eaten with manicured pinkies. Beverages included flutes of caviar smoothies and flights of oyster juice. The fountain centerpiece: Two mini-waterfalls of Charles Lafitte Rosé and Beaujolais cascading to a riptide that funneled into a glass ant farm basin. (The tide of cheap champagne and bad wine flushed in and out, back and forth through the tunnels of sand.)

Washed out actor **Vince Vaughn** was Master of Ceremonies. Vaughn unveiled a masterpiece to mark the occasion and adorn the modern wing. It was the pinnacle of the party: two glass statues of Ken Griffin and his wife **Anne**—whom he met in 2003 at 872 North State Street just off the Red Line.

The billionaire twosome (or threesome when they brought their nanny into the mix) was acclaimed for their charitable ventures, which included buying the abstract oil painting "False Start" for their personal collection. (They would later learn it was finger-painted by **Jasper Johns**, a 10-month old child from the Abrakadoodle Art Studio for Kids in Singapore.) For a mere $80 million, the frugal art lovers purchased "False Start," which hangs today above the lovers' gilded conscience.

In '06 the Griffins donated $19 million to the Art Institute for its new wing. The Griffin glass statues are nudes—the curves chipped in all the right spots. When you position the statues *just so*, the sunlight reflecting off Lake Michigan ricochets into the gallery and shoots prisms across the couple's sensually opened mouths—as if they are eating air bubbles of rainbows.

The Griffin statues are adjoined at their rear ends like pygopagus twins—Anne's perked up slightly in mid-twerk. The statues are ornamented with glass cockatoos mating in a glass puddle at the Griffins' calloused feet.

Just as Vaughn uncovered the billionaires, the 240,000 Democrats crashed the bedding. The riot was helmed by Emanuel and avid Clinton (Hillary) supporter **Owen Wilson**. Talk about anarchy at the Art Institute! There was pushing and punching. Kicking and screaming. Hair pulling and teasing. Tearing up floorboards and running with slivers.

Chicago celebrity **Oprah Winfrey**—who was fighting alongside Emanuel and Wilson—hoisted a giant gray bean off the buffet and *hurled* it at the glass ant farm. (In litigation later—the suit concerned the collanteral damage of whole families—Winfrey claimed she had thought the bean was an innocuous cloud, incapable of insecticidal impact.)

The finely catered food—fresh and impartially digested—went flying in the air without owner. Ultimately, the Democrats (in "Yes We Can United!" apparel) and the Republicans (in nighties *marching* with lucky liberated ants) clashed at the tip of the Ken statue's foremost cockatoo. At this point, a now sickly salami—stuck to the ceiling—unclenched its sticky grip and splattered on Ken's head-given cockatoo—lubricating its stiffness with meat fat. The greasy moisture and weighty bulk (the salami came from Costco) broke *3 billion shards into a puddle of glass*. (The Griffin statues remain on exhibit today, but the Ken statue's groin is prudently covered with a food stamp.)

The political pajama party was a bust, and the once hopeful Ken withdrew without further incident. The "Art Institute Riot" secured Emanuel's spot as a brave, no-nonsense leader. Emanuel himself has hinted at a possible 2020 presidential run. "I will reveal my decision," Emanuel stated in '15, "at a place no man has ever been: The Smith Museum of Stained Glass Windows at Chicago's Navy Pier. *And,* I will boldly invite Winfrey as a gesture to symbolize how trust conquers fragility."

THE DEBATES

Mount Rushmore Face-Off

Flash back to the '08 election debates. Remember when **John McCain** called in sick with a grin ache? Well, Romney (then age 61) stepped in as Interim Debater to "take on" the ambitious young senator from Illinois. (Romney was not intimidated. He had revealed his acting chops in the Cranbrook School's rendition of "Hair" in 1963.) Romney figured if he won McCain the debate, he'd be a poster boy for 2012.

Obama was highly regarded as an eloquent speaker. It appeared a no-brainer that Obama would win the '08 debates, and subsequently, the presidency. It seemed *such a sure thing* that sculptors started carving Obama's face into Mount Rushmore—between **Thomas Jefferson** and **Theodore Roosevelt**. (The sculptors applied the "Sideism" technique, in which a sculpture is created vertically from left to right. This method originated in the late 1950s—devised by a company of Venetian blinds artists gone rogue—who, of their own accord—regularly met on the side in the shade under the Bridge of Sides to hone their gills.)

Just before the first debate, the sculptors had completed 50% of the carving. The complete left half of Obama's face was finely sculpted. To America's astonishment, during the 1st debate Obama entered a mysterious trance...rendered speechless. (Obama later explained he had been having a flashback to his pot-smoking daze and was picturing himself in a "white classmate's sparkling new van.") Romney won the first debate, and everyone commended McCain on such a great job.

Panicked, the sculptors carved the right half of Romney's face into the granite—adjoining Obama's left. The finished (frankly frightening) face was christened "Romama." In 2009, **Margo Lion**, co-chair of the president's Committee of Arts and Humanities (CAH), ordered a federal engineer to affix an enormous rope from behind Romama's ears that ties behind its head like a Halloween mask. To this day, Lion insists it's a safety measure to keep the rock from falling. (But the vast populace believes it was a bipartisan attempt to save face.)

...Legend has it Jefferson and Roosevelt have edged slightly away from Romama's face—in fear or perhaps embarrassment.

A Staged Debate

Back to the 2012 election: Stewart takes it upon himself.

The U.S. Constitution's 39th Amendment (*Bill of Rights*, Appendix F) states that *a minimum of two* presidential debates must take place even if "there be-ith one sole man, standing alone, by himself, with no other, on his own, stag."

To satisfy this technicality, Stewart teamed up with Apple® to help him secure the job by undertaking the technical specs. So Apple® invented the nation's first "Online Town Hall Forum"—a program that yielded fruitful results. The forum's moderator was the flirtatious voice of **Samantha from "Sex in the City."** (In 2010 Samantha also whored her voice as a Manhattan GPS orator—downloadable for $12.95.) Online spectators voted for their winner by text *(standard text messaging rates may be waived)*, and Stewart won the debate by his lonesome by a landslide.

The second debate was a one-man show—"performance art" style format. It took place at the tiny, avant-garde Kraine Theater in Manhattan, and was moderated by performance artist **Laurie Anderson**. Stewart—wearing black tights and a turtle neck—role-played *both* himself *and* his opponent. A soft white spotlight turned off and then on whenever he switched characters.

Stewart would have received a standing ovation if the poor theater's ceiling had been high enough. Republicans, however, stooped to complain it was a biased debate because Stewart enacted the world's most annoying persona—**Jar Jar Binks**—as his imaginary opponent.

Ryan Regresses
The '12 Vice Presidential debate was scheduled to air October 11 on ABC at 6 p.m. Pacific in Kentucky. Veep nominee Colbert—freshly preened and powdered—slid his fingers through his hair and dampened his nape with gel. The sprucely clad candidate—a dapper 48-years young—chalked and fondled his hands in anticipatory eagerness to impel himself upon viewers. Colbert was slotted to face off against then-Congressional Representative **Paul Ryan**, a whimpersnapper farm-boy from Spread Eagle, Wisconsin, where his mother **Betty** nursed him into politics.

But when the moderator, **Martha Radasstz**, beat the gong with her mallet, Ryan was nowhere to be weaned. Rumors ran rampant: Was Ryan not running? Was Ryan on the run? Did Ryan have the runs? Would Ryan return or relinquish his race? Without even parting his lips, Colbert was awarded the win, left speechless in brazen bashfulness. The next morning, a Republican search party—on a quest to save Ryan—located him in private. The congressman was in a tight corner, feverishly suckling a bottle of water. Ryan came clean and confessed his addiction to pure liquid hydrogen and oxygen—sapping his political future and tapping his mother's teat.

STEWART'S INAUGURATION AND EXECUTIVE OUTFIT

The Assassination Attempt and the Spaceballs Alien

On Monday, January 21, 2013 Jonathan "Stu" Leibowitz Stewart—aside his wife, **Tracey Big-MacShane** and ex-wife **Annie**—was sworn in as President of the United States.

The adrenaline-pumping part of the event was the shotgun assassination attempt on Stewart by a bow-tied, once 35-year old man on air. Stewart was caught in the crossfire, but saved by CNN executives who threw a towel in at the stumbling gunman, tripping up his aim. The would-be assassin was identified as **Tucker Carlson**. Defense unsuccessfully argued that Carlson was just implementing his Daily task list in bullet points. But the judge didn't see it that day. Carlson was made to sit in the back row as punishment and deprived of sweets for a week.

Upon taking the motels.com-sponsored oath on a dresser drawer Bible, panic ensued over who would sing the National Anthem. **Janet Jackson** had been slotted to perform, but Security stopped her at the metal detectors—citing a war-drone malfunction and frisking for proof (founded). Fortunately, actor **John Hurt** was in inaugural attendance, and, as luck would have it, **the alien** who had made a cameo in **Mel Brooks'** "Spaceballs" (1987) burst through Hurt's abdomen, jumped up on the platform, and commenced singing "hello my ragtime gal" in top hat with cane.

Colbert's Silent Tongue

On January 21, 2013, Colbert's first day as VPOTUS, former Veep Biden reservedly handed over the keys to the Naval Observatory—home to Vice Presidents and their 2nd ladies since 1974. (VPs grumble, however, that the navels are frequently covered up with bulky sweaters, obliging the men to strain their eyeballs and imaginations. Historically, belly balling is a vice Veeps view as vital.)

Colbert showed up bright and early on his first day—after a restful night of inaugural ball hopping. He swiped his keycard to enter the White House; punched in at the Grand Staircase time-clock; and proceeded to the State Dining Room for his complimentary continental breakfast or, at the very least, a steamy cup of joe. (Colbert had seen "Downton Abbey"; he knew how this worked.) But, oh my! Delectables and coffee were nowhere to be seen! However, when he spotted the dinner gong, he rubbed his hands happily together. That would do the trick! Just as Colbert was about to strike, he slipped on a stick of butter and hit his head on the bell. The gong was deafening.

Colbert regained consciousness at the White House nurse's office 24-hours later in real time. He awoke his usual irreverent self, but when he opened his mouth to ask what ridiculous trauma transpired, he was overcome with a fear of public speaking. Colbert choked on his words. He needed the Heimlich to even force out a "hello"!

President Stewart arrived for the nurse's report, which described Colbert's vernacularly catatonic condition. Stewart gasped, remembering that the VP's commencement speech at WA's Walla Walla College's D.C. Extension was within the hour! Stewart consulted with strategic advisors **Donald O'Connor** and **Gene Kelly**, and the three came up with a brilliant idea:

1.) Stewart hires a charismatic male speaker.
2.) Colbert stands on stage at Walla Walla and lip-synchs his script.
3.) The charismatic man behind the curtain delivers the speech.

Stewart made a call, and, faster than the speed of frightening, **Bill O'Reilly** was at the door—ready for rehearsal.

The curtain stunt worked so seamlessly that Stewart contracted O'Reilly to do Colbert voiceovers at *all* VP speaking events. Funny thing is, it turns out Colbert and O'Reilly were *already* working this scheme for "The Colbert Report." Really the only people who know Colbert's true voice are his wife, kids, and whoever watched Colbert's first feature film "Let it Snow" (1999).

Stewart's Cabinet Unhinged

Choosing the right cabinet is a challenge we all deal with: be it our starter house, our timeshare, or our first presidency. Fortunately, White Home Depot is there to help—with a diverse array of in-stock and custom-made choices. The first step, White Home Depot says, is to ask yourself: What kind of Cabinet can I sleep with and what will my Budget allow?

SOS!
To start, Stewart selected Conan O'Brien as his Secretary of State. Stewart deemed O'Brien "a stand up gentleman—civilized and well-red." The comedians had made amends after their infamous "I Heart Applebees" feud in '08 in which (under Colbert's watchful guard) they fisticuffed over which one of them could eat the most backbone. O'Brien was also in need of a boost to which Stewart was sympathetic. (O'Brien's wife, Elizabeth, had deserted their marriage and kids to serve as make-out artist for Powell on "American Idol"—leaving O'Brien in the trying role of solo dad.)

An ecstatic O'Brien got the big news just as he was cementing his footprint in the Hollywood Walk of Fame. In jubilation, he raced across the country by foot (weighted down with residual cement) to accept the post—camera crew at his side. He reached D.C. in under an hour, but, unfortunately, O'Brien only lasted seven months as SOS—likely due to the physical toll of running across the country with blocks of cement on his feet. O'Brien was so exhausted he could only perform his job functions remotely via Skype on his Lenovo. Stewart looked the other way as long as he could, but his neck couldn't take it any longer when Internet censorship in Uzbekistan interfered with O'Brien's diplomatic dinner with President **Islam Karimov**.

With O'Brien off the screen, Stewart scrambled to find a new SOS. He considered enlisting buoyant personalities **Al Gore** or **John Kerry**. But Gore was finishing the last sketch of his run in a Cheatham County Community Theater production of "The Ice Man Commeth," and Kerry, to the nation's astonishment, was leaving politics to open a "My Little Pony®" gift shop at the Fresh Pond Mall in Cambridge.

In desperation, Stewart placed a "Help Wanted" ad in the *Village Voice* classifieds which listed the job requirements. In 2012 *Village Voice* classifieds ran $70 for 40 words. Due to budgetary cuts, Stewart trimmed the ad down to 15 words for $50—eliminating the phone screen and the prerequisite the secretary type 65 words a minute. The vacancy was eventually filled out by **Dolly Parton**, whose only demand was to work a 9-to-5 (Eastern) schedule.

Second Class Secretaries
Having secured Parton in his grip, Stewart appointed the following non-perishables to his cabinet:

Press Secretary—**Dear Abby**
Secretary of the Interior—**Elle Décor**
Secretary of Transportation—**Miss Daisy**
Secretary of Energy—**Dietrich Mateschitz** (Founder of Red Bull GmbH)
Secretary of Defense—**Fred Gailey** (Santa Claus's defense attorney in 1947's "Miracle on 34th Street")
Secretary of the Treasury—**Captain Jack Sparrow**
Secretary of Veteran Affairs—**John McCain**
Secretary of Housing and Urban Development—**Eminem** (Chocolate manufacturer, not to be confused with wrapper)
Attorney General—**The Marlboro Man**

Secretary of Agriculture:
Stewart struggled with filling this fertile post. His first choice: Greek mythology's **Demeter**, Goddess of Agriculture. But Demeter was only available six months of the year (citing family matters). Disheartened by the whole "temperamental goddess" thing, Stewart considered inviting **John Franklin** (child actor in 1984's "Children of the Corn") to step into the row. (The Administration wouldn't question Franklin about his questionable background check—given his character Isaac was a minor at the time of the event in question.) Finally, Stewart fixed himself on enclosing an earthly woman: He presented SOA to **Andrew Wyeth's Christina,** who rose to the occasion to accept the position.

(For a full list of Stewart's secretaries, see calluspas.com.)

Samantha's Bees and John's Olives

President Stewart—with the futile help of Shepherd's Woodworks, Inc. in Lubbock—had difficulty recruiting and retaining a staff of solid support. After a 37-minute wait in line, Stewart succeeded in getting Best Bed and Beyond's® Geek Squad to extend their reach to headhunting via their pillow division. The Geek Squad attempted to woo Stewart's former "Daily Show" cohort **Samantha Bee** as Sting Operations Manager. (Responsibilities included spying under covers at the Scripps

National Spelling Bee to catch cheaters.) But Bee was stuck on becoming an astronaut—filling the spacesuit of **Buzz Aldrin** and *ful*filling his mission to discover a Bit O'Honey® in Mars®.

The Geek Squad approached another "Daily Show" newscaster: **John Oliver**. Oliver cheerfully accepted the grim position of International Director of the Division of Family, Child Services and Transportation (DFCST). Sadly, Oliver's first assignment became his last.

Stewart had assigned Oliver the diplomatic task of trying to sway **Vladimir Putin's** mind about the (then) recently-passed Russian legislation which prohibits Americans from adopting Russian children and highways. On behalf of an anonymous American couple who had adopted a much-needed highway in Kamchatka—only to have the deal null and void!—Oliver flew to Kamchatka (which cannot be reached by road). His mission: To pave the way to an agreement with the Russians to bring the highway back to its documented U.S. home.

Oliver, when in Rome (FCO transfer to PKC) caught wind of a Moscowian child abuse scandal involving corporal punishment at the Kremlin's military orphanage. Oliver made a surprise guest appearance at the orphanage (PKC to DME) to politely interrogate the manager about the facility's childrearing practices.

Oliver's Russian translation of "Please Sir, I want some more (information)" came out as "Никогда не позвольте мне уезжать, даже если я спрашиваю к." Loosely translated in English, this means "Never let me leave even if I ask to." To this day, the Kremlin's orphanage is holding Oliver without release. He is under the strict watch of **Miss Hannigan**, who orders him to spear toothpicks with olives for her bathwater gin martinis.

The Incorporation of Congress and the Inferiority Complex of the SEC

During the Stewart presidency, the nation underwent a dramatic restructuring of its political body: the merger of the U.S. Senate and the U.S. House of Representatives. Since 1789, the two entities had operated as independent subsidiaries of their umbrella company, Congress. In 2014, the C-levels of Congress made the "executive" decision to merge the subsidiaries into one corporation. (Its business entity title: "Incorporated Congress of the United States.") The corporation went public on the New York Stock Exchange in the summer of '15 under the ticker ICUS and shares have since shot though the dome. ICUS is also traded on the London and Paris stock exchanges under the tickers ICENGLAND, ICFRANCE.

The merger resulted in great strife for—and the ultimate demise of—the ailing Securities Exchange of Currency (and Baseball Cards) (SEC(BC)). The SEC(BC) was ill-prepared for the influx of insider trading. Nor were they prepared for **Gordon Gekko's** return in the "Occupy Wall Street" sequel. The SEC(BC) suffered total meltdown. They stopped cashing checks, exchanging currency, giving loans on payday, and issuing vehicle stickers. Feeling vulnerable, the chairmen regrouped to form the Insecurities Exchange Commission (IEC). Today, the IEC has two functions: 1.) to service self-complex sufferers without self-sufficient support, and 2.) to handle a hotline for struggling salesmen who work on commission.

Baseball cards were left entirely out of the equation.

Part II

ROMANTIC ESCAPADES AND THE NSA

The Sexting Scandal of Petraeus and Paula

During Stewart's term there were scandals galore—the most titillating involved former CIA (Conspicuous Infidelity Agency) director **David Petraeus**. While in his post, Petraeus (a married man) would ritually rollerblade with his biographer **Paula Abdul** in Afghanistan.

However, their Yahoo! greeting e-card exchanges were leaked—the content bursting with innuendos. So the NSA (Not So Anonymous) began monitoring Petraeus's and Abdul's texting data. The first confiscated text was a message to Petraeus from Abdul that read "I8U." The NSA misinterpreted the "8,"—thinking Abdul meant "I hate you." But NSA director **John C. Linglis's** teenage son poked his head into the matter to explain the text's meaning was "I ate you." This intimation Linglis found quite cunning, and an even *greater* threat which clearly involved cannibalism. However, Petraeus's texted reply to

Abdul read "U can 8 me, if I can 8 U." The NSA smelled something fishy, and—assuming something was up—thenceforth collected all of the twosome's texts—which NSA's computer lab technician decoded.

Text Transcript Petraeus/Abdul – Exchanged Spring 2012

ABDUL: **SHH (69)**
Secret Meeting

PETRAEUS: **UR ^ MYN ^?**
Your place or mine?

ABDUL: **HM-BN@UR^**
Never been to yours

PETRAEUS: **I :O! IF U :O**!
I'll show you mine if you show me yours

ABDUL: **U #&*(@ ---> .... ;)**
You are a naughty soldier…I like it

PETRAEUS: **MY--'>***U**
My pistol is cocked for you

ABDUL: **BAM et al – WEE…**
All guns and no play…

PETRAEUS: ****POW**
Shoot

ABDUL: **I?\UR $**
I thought that was your job

PETRAEUS: **N! IM ****POW 8^… :(**
No, I mean shoot, wife's here…sorry

ABDUL: **K _ (US)**
OK, keep us under cover

PETRAEUS: **BYOB?**
See you at the mosque tomorrow night?

ABDUL: **I@BOO! U/M ( ) ."[{}]" oo!**
I'll wear a mask! We'll have our own little "mosquerade" ball!

PETRAEUS: **LOL(IYH)**
Laugh out loud (in your head)

And so, Petraeus resigned from the CIA. Today Petraeus is *Head Counsel of Camp Counselors* of the Boy Scouts of America, and steers the Bring the Scouts to the Middle East (BSME) initiative.

E-Dating Hackers Spread Virus

STDs went viral in the fall of '14 when online dating websites were hacked by the outfit Virtual Afflictions Group (VAG). It turns out the VAG masterminds had been devising this hack-job for over a decade. There were early signs of suspicious activity—dating back to the late nineties upon the founding of Match.com.

In 2003, the FBHI (Federal Bureau of Hacker Investigations) supplied (then) President **George W. Bush** with Intelligence that agents had discovered a deserted makeshift computer lab with suspicious vials of viruses. The FBHI reported signs of "weapons of Match destruction" to the president. Bush, however, was incapable of processing the Intelligence, and led the nation to war.

The virus was catastrophic to the single and the married-guys-pretending-to-be-single (MGPTBS) communities. The STD ("Singles to Destruction") virus worked like this: whenever the dating website user sent an electronic "wink" to another user, that wink carried a Hermes virus that delivered messages between the Clods and Portals. The messages contained traces of Mercury—transmitting toxic chemicals. Circuits crisscrossed and mass infected major cities. Then the circuits came to towns.

Soon all the users' profiles experienced "pins and needles sensations" ("Mercury Poisoning," *Cases Journal, 2009*) and lost their electronic libido. One user reported that—since his online profile got infected with Mercury—"after having sex I feel very run down and some of my symtoms [symptoms] get a little worst [worse]" ("Sex and Mercury Poisoning," *anonymous, Orbis Vitare Forum.com*).

Disillusioned with dating websites, singles and MGPTBS blew up their online accounts with F-bombs, and turned to *It's Just Punch* ® to fill their voids. At *It's Just Punch* (a face-to-face dating service), matchmakers set up innocent luncheons for love-starved professionals. Thanks to *It's Just Punch*, singles and MGPTBS could meet without the sexual awkwardness that alcoholic drinks at bars inevitably provoke: "Oooh, she thinks I'm witty!" "Will he ever shut up?" "Oooh, I think she's going to let me kiss her!" "Eewww, his lips look like skinned seals."

VAG, however, reconstructed to form PNIS (Party of No Interest in Sobriety). The Party concocted a chemical formula CH_3CH_2OH to spike punch by means of airborne parasites. PNIS injected the parasites with ethanol and a sharpened sweet tooth—attracting the bugs to *hosts serving singles punch*. In 2016, *It's Just Punch* shuddered due to an influx of bitter sexual harassment lawsuits. The claim: Staggering MGPTBS were subjected to repeated punches by tipsy women, causing serious injury to the men's egos and storylines.

GLOBAL FRICTION AND OTHER TALES OF DISASTERS

The Amazon Plant Invasion

In 2013, man-eating Venus Fly Traps invaded the Amazon jungle. The carnivorous plants grew to gorilla size—getting bigger and bigger with each crunchy insect and small furry mammal they ate. By 2014 the plants were devouring jaguars and cougars crossing over the hills. But the plants' thirst for blood was still unquenched. By 2015 they began to threaten the Amazon's human population, which was 188,000 according to the 2010 census. (A 2014 Amazon census was conducted, but the door-to-door census taker and his notebook went unaccounted for.)

Amazons retaliated by wearing "Don't Feed the Plants" t-shirts. When that attire flopped, Amazons inebriated the plants by pouring a great deal of red vine down their traps—in hopes the plants would think it was blood. But the vine was actually good for the plants' hearts, and they grew *even stronger*.

America stepped in. President Stewart sent naval ships across the ocean to the Amazon, saving 50% on shipping by placing the executive order online. The ship was giftwrapped and labeled "SIRLOIN." The plants clapped their traps together excitedly and pulled the drawstring. Out sprang the U.S. Navy in full combat mode—Trojan Horse style, but in tanks due to the humidity. The naval combatants slew the plants with tear gas. The traps—and a few innocent bystander willows—wilted in their defeat.

The Amazons expressed their gratitude by granting the strapping sailors tankless gratification with the hot giantess Wonder Woman. The grieving willows were granted tissues for their weepy hollow.

An Infestation of Tics Down Under

A tic infestation in Australia made headlines in 2013. The cause of the infestation: Australian Aborigines released the tics in rage upon the revelation that **Jeff Fratt**, of "The Wiggles," lied about his aboriginal origins. Fratt had claimed he was of Aussie Aborigine descent, but was, in fact, an Aborigine from Tahiti. You see, Fratt had been pulled over by authorities (for sleeping at the wheel of his big red car) on Wanneroo Road. They popped the trunk only to find Fratt's Tahitian passport alongside some monoi oil and noni.

The tics spread throughout the Australian continent—which some argue is not one. Now all Australians are nervously shrugging their shoulders in jerky, choppy motions. Australians heed the UN (United Neuroses) annually at general assemblies—imploring the UN to mandate international research to identify a cure. But the UN clearly doesn't take them seriously. The diplomats from down under keep shrugging jerkily—so it's generally assumed the Aussies are indifferent to their own entreaty. Australian scientists have tried to invent a cure *themselves*, but their incessant shrugging causes them to drop their beakers, spilling chemicals onto their sneakers—hence not getting anywhere unscathed.

Empathetic to the hassle of tics down under, President Stewart has assured Australian Prime Minister **Elvis Abbot** that he will meet with him personally (where Elvis lives) to ponder potential presidential preferential treatments in May. (In May DCA/SYD flights are the most economical on Expedia and CheapTics.com.)

McDonalds Serves Freedom Flies

In May 2012, U.S./France relations hit a cul de sac when the French people elected **François Hollande** as their President. Hollande's allegiance to the Socialist Party stirred—what came to be known as—"The Mold War." McDonalds Corporation took patriotic action by changing the name of their "French Fries" to "Freedom Fries."

However, McDonalds' copywriter committed a grave typo on the new menus. When typing "Fries," she accidentally hit the "L" key instead of the "R." Over 14,000 McDonalds' restaurants advertised they served "Freedom Flies." To make matters worse, the same copywriter committed *another* typo by adding an "S" to "OIL." McDonalds' new menus boasted they fried their flies in "Vegetable Soil." (The copywriter also accidentally omitted salads from the menu, but was relieved when no one noticed.)

As a result, the Department of Shelf and Cumin Services (DOSACS)—charged with the inspection of infested facilities, moldy sauce and spices—intervened. DOSACS inspectors inspected the menu, and concluded "yes," the fast food was beset with insects and mold. DOSACS prohibited McDonalds from selling fries and placed an order to replace McDonalds' vegetable oil with Hollandaise sauce.

Consequently, McDonalds suffered a financial wallop, and as a cost-cutting measure, stopped stuffing toys in Happy Meals. But The Mold War ended in 2014 when **Gérard Depardieu** made a big appearance in the film "Welcome to New York." McDonalds regained market share by offering its gourmet "Joe of Arch" coffee, "McSalad Niçoise," and "McFoie Gras Burgers."

The Study Abroad Tax Evasion Scandal

For decades the IRS (Inmate Release Service) looked the other way in the face of evasion. But in 2015, the Brain Industry Association (BIA) forced the IRS to collect taxes from clever study-abroad students working as waiters. The order stemmed from Intelligence that American college students—working under the table—were suffering repeated concussions due to bumping their heads when their shifts were up.

The IRS flew assessors in to assess the situation. The assessors frequented a multitude of eating establishments such as *Hofbräuhaus* in München (Munich); the *Brasserie Julien* in Paris (Paris), *Restaurante Figueira Rubaiyat* in São Paulo (San Paulo), and 餓的孩子 in 香港 (Hong Kong).

The American students were difficult to locate, but after months of being forced to smell the fat assessors' feet, the students couldn't bear it anymore. They tied the assessors' shoelaces together to trip them up, and escaped from under the tables—bumping their heads on the way.

The Clothing of Guantanamo

In 2015, President Stewart mandated the closing of the Guantanamo Detention Center at the naval base in Cuba. (Stewart was in the 'hood on a musical pursuit of Havana sitars.) The Administration's intent was to transfer the Guantanamo prisoners to U.S. correctional facilities in Coal County, WV in order to expand their mines.

One prisoner put up a major fuss: **Robert Opel**. Opel was imprisoned for streaking at the 46th Academy Awards ceremony in 1974 behind actor **David Niven**. Opel quite fancied the Guantanamo facilities, and had even taken to wearing bed sheet togas. He rallied his fellow inmates to protest the closing by going on an underwear strike and setting themselves on fire by self-flatulation.

The prisoners' efforts were flamefully feeble. In 2016, the U.S. government hired actress-turned-NASA (National Alien Slayer Agency) contractor **Sigourney Weaver** to tackle the shackled. Weaver donned an oxygen helmet and buckled into a mechanical robot suit (courtesy of Caterpillar®) to thwart the naked, unlucky strikers. Weaver succeeded in stuffing the men back into their jumpsuits. She extinguished their sparks with slime, but not before roasting some Stay Puft Marshmallows® first.

As punishment, a weary, worn-out Opel was sentenced to a weak in solitary consignment.

Italy Loses Color

In fall 2014, a perplexing—but somehow romantic—occurrence occurred in Italy. (To this very day the phenomenon remains unexplained.) We're talking, of course, about when Italy turned black and white. The first signs—in the summer of '14—were barely noticeable: Italians reported a "La sfumatura dolce grigia nell'aria." (Translation: "slighty grayish hue in the air.") And "Questi giorni il mio accantona sempre Dusty di sguardo." (Translation: "These days my shelves always look dusty.")

But come October, it was as clear as cliché: When people crossed the border into Italy (including Sicily and Sardinia) color vanishes. All of Italy (except San Marino and the Vatican City) is in black and white—and sometimes skips a little, like an old foreign film.

Opponents of the bizarre manifestation were primarily Italian businesspersons serving the tourism industry. The sporadic skipping of Italy—like an old reel of silent film playing—dislodged the Tower of Pisa. The tower toppled atop a tourist shop, dislodging hundreds of miniature ceramic Towers of Pisa off the seemingly-dusty shelves. "What will fall to ruins next!" tour guides complained in vexation, "the Roman Coliseum?!?!"

The Venice Travel Bureau was especially rattled. "Who wants to ride a gondola on canals that look like oil?" the Bureau complained. Today Venetian tourism barely stays afloat; and is at the mere mercy of Turkish, Bulgarian and Romanian tourists—and other vacationers indigenous to the coastal countries along the Black Sea.

Some Italians are actually proponents of the change. For example, old movie buffs and fans of **Federico Fellini's** "8 ½" and "La Dolce Vita"; and the small-minded, who prefer to see things in black and white. Also, there is disinterest among another group of *Cittadini italiani*. In 2015, Italians who are already colorblind released this statement: "NON RIESCO davvero a vedere che cosa l'affare grande." (Translation: "I really don't see what the big deal is.")

The Controversial Erection of the BOLLYWOOD Sign in Tirumala

To honor Hindi cinema and the old Bombay, the Indian movie-making industry erected a gigantic sign of letters that read "BOLLYWOOD"—modeled after the famous Hollywood sign in California. The BOLLYWOOD letters were delivered, assembled and up-raised by a collection of children. The chore was filmed documentary-style by British director **Danny Boyle** ("Plum Paw Pill Pun Pear," "Brain-Clotting").

When the BOLLYWOOD sign was erected in 2014—by the all-but-underarm sweat of child labor—the sign's dimensions measured—like its California counterpart—45-ft. tall and 350-ft. long. The glittering new landmark was strewn with blinking multi-colored Christmas lights and decked with mini-speakers playing Bhangra pop. The BOLLYWOOD sign, oh how it graced the rolling hills of Tirumala!

Upon the release of Boyle's documentary: "A Sign of Good Hill Bunting" (2015), word spread that the children had not been paid for their labor. Humanitarian activists and stage moms—from all parts of the world—flew to Tirumala to protest. They stormed the hill; dismantled the gigantic sign; and hacked it to pieces with machetes and baseball bats. BOLLYWOOD was annihilated.

In the calm after the storm, the Indian movie-making industry negotiated a re-erection of the sign. The entertainment executives agreed to rehire the children and—this time around—pay them with compliments and Boost®.

Part III

DOMESTICATED NUISANCES AND A CRAZY LITTLE THING CALLED WAR

Giving America the New Bird

On August 28, 2013, a bold body of bald men marched on Washington—protesting funding cuts in hair regrowth research. They stomped atop tens of thousands of 1 dollar bills—to symbolize the government's historical favoritism of bourgeois, bushy-rooted American men—like **George Washington** with his lush white locks.

"My dear folk, please do not hold me accountable: In 1782, America chose the Bald Eagle as its symbol of moral character," President Stewart exclaimed at an emergency press conference. "Therefore, the Bald American People should revel in pride! They should stand tall, beaming in their shine. Alas, today's march affirms that bald Americans do not take this stance."

The press conference's court reporter, **Brenda Starr,** pointed out: "Perhaps the protesters are offended by the Bald Eagle's imminent extinction,"—typing her words as she spoke.

The president proclaimed that perfectly plausible, and—to appease the men's furry—Stewart appointed a new national bird: The African Grey Parrot.

This sophisticated feathered friend has been called the "perfect mix of brains and beauty" (*Bird Talk*, Aug. '92) and the "Cadillac of parrots" (*Bird Talk*, Sept. '93).

Stewart received wide-spread support. After all, the Cadillac was an American car—a division of the Ford Motor Company. The rechristening was fowlproof!

And so the African Grey Parrot became the new emblem of American patriotism: A symbol of a changing demographic with a charming sense of parrody.

The Fraggles' Fuss about Fracking

In '15, the famous fracking site of Fellsmere, Fl. furnished a flabbergasting finding, not unlike the fossils found in Pompeii, Pa. The hydraulic-fracking miners injected the flammable fluid into the site's squeaky floorboards and inserted a vacuum through the crack to suck up fossil fuel. To the miners' amazement, the nozzle guzzled the *fossil* but not the fuel.

What the miners retrieved from the rock was, in fact, the remains of **Boober Fraggle**—the beloved puppet from **Jim Henson's** "Fraggle Rock" (1983-1987). The dead Fraggle's encrusted arms were extended—one stuck mid-wave. Poor Boober no longer resembled his early self: blue-green complexion, orange mop of hair, animated essence—gone without a trace. No, Boober's felt was soaked with soot, his hair wriggled with worms, his eyes popped out of their sockpuppets. (Given that Boober Fraggle never had eyes to begin with, forensics confirmed the puppet's identity without subjecting the furry corpse to frenetic testing.)

The finding of the exhumed Fraggle ignited outrage among Former Fraggle Followers (FFF). Chants of "Fracking is a folly!"; "Don't frack until you're ready!"; "Burial for Boober!" and "We're not your puppets!" filled the air in Washington.

In an attempt to appease the mob, President Stewart alerted FFF to the fact that he *himself* was a Jim Henson fan—citing **Miss Piggy's** guest appearance on "The Daily Show" in 1999 and his own debut on "Sesame Street" (2007, Episode 4,156). Fraggle purists were not pacified. They argued that—despite design by the same maker—Muppets were a different breed.

But FFF eased off when Stewart granted Boober a proper burial—no strings attached. The funeral procession was aired live on HBO and CBC (Canada). The scene was somber and poignant—an American flag draped over the casket case in which Boober lay.

The Mississippi Missile Crisis

No American will forget the Mississippi Missile Crisis in October 2013. It began when a naval officer and a gentlewoman met on the Biloxi wharf. The officer picked up on her classy airs, and—for a pick-me-up—invited her to biscuits and tea as a pickup. During their herbal tryst, the officer received a call on his walkie talkie from his commanders.

Knowing it's improper to take a call during tea, the officer whispered into his walkie: "Can't talk. Time for lunch. Holding hot bread. Biloxi bomb shell. Sweater tight. Nude-colored slacks. Wow. I'll ask if she's got a sister. (Murmur.) She don't. Will be late tomorrow morning at the ship. Yowza!!!"

The static clinging to the line caused the commanders to hear: "Can't talk. Time for launch. Holding me hostage. Biloxi bombs and shells. Better fight. Nuclear attack. Ow. I'll ask if they'll stop the missile. (Murmur.) They won't. Kill at 8 tomorrow morning or I'm whipped. Ouch, ahhh!!!"

When President Stewart caught wind of the Mississippi missiles, he commanded the <u>Defensive Ministry of Violence</u> (DMV) to reposition its nuclear telescope 1,276 km NW to target Biloxi. The president ordered a warning missile fired to show Mississippi that the U.S. meant business.

The missile penetrated an abandoned bomb shelter built by visionaries during the Civil War. Barrels of baked beans exploded—spraying airborne debris across all of Harrison County. Mississippians cheered, fetched their banjoes, and circled 'round the campfire—roasting weenies and shooting the breeze. It took 13 days to clean up the mess.

After FEMA had rung out its massive mop, Mississippi was deemed safe, and DMV's nuclear telescope repositioned itself sturdily back to Aruba.

A Crockpot of Bull and the Texas Secession

Since 1885 Texas had been dying to secede from the Union. Secession petitions are reviewed by the president only when the petitioning entity produces a minimum of 25,000 signatures in one day.

(This requirement was put in place by 1st POTUS, George Washington—persuaded by his bff **John Hancock** to sign the policy into effect. In 1910, President **William Taft** added an appendix to the law that permitted electronic signatures and "Likes" as valid tallies. Some speculate Taft was sucking up to **Thomas Edison** who owned the Edison's Electronic Write Company and invented the sociable media platform for the telegraph. Others say Taft added the appendix as a cautionary measure should he lose his.)

On December 29, 2015, the State of Texas's Facebook "Petition for an Independent Texas" page received the 25,000 "Likes" it needed to be acknowledged by President Stewart. The State was startled by just how quickly Stewart acquiesced to their plea. On December 30, 2015, President Stewart awoke to circumcise Texas from the U.S. just after showering.

Boy, was *that* a painful operation! Before **Melissa and Doug**® could redesign their "Deluxe Wooden USA Map Puzzle"®, many technicalities had to be pieced together. Namely, San Antonio and Austin. The two cities were in a tizzy about "this whole secession thing." Their combined 2,225,543 (and one-on-the-way) population did not *want* to be snipped off from their mother country.

President Stewart presented two options:
1. San Antonions and Austonions could give the new Republic of Texas a shot—like the remaining 23,833,660 (and one-on-the-way-out) of the gun-slaphappy Texans—and embrace their puns and clay pigeons.

2. Texans could build a 49-ft. wall around both cities. San Antonio and Austin would be designated U.S. Commonwealths—granted the right to vote in U.S. elections. The stipulation: Texas's 38 electoral votes would be divided equally between the liberal Commonwealths.

In the end, San Antonio opted to relinquish their U.S. citizenship, and Austin opted for the wall. Requirements included:
1. "The Austin City Limits" radio show had to be brought within city limits.

2. San Antonio could keep Waxy O'Connor's Irish Pub on the Riverwalk, but the Alamo had to go. Its Texas ties were just too trite. Plus it was a landmark of a famous piece of U.S. history: **Davy Crocker's** patriotic mechanical bull showdown against **Al Capone**. (Crocker later married baker **Betty**, an American icon in her own bite.)

On February 14, 2016—around breakfast time—the U.S. airlifted the Alamo to Birmingham, Alabamo. But after doing so, the U.S. realized they really didn't know what to do with the darn thing. Americans were disappointed. It was much smaller than it looked in the postcards.

So—around dinner time—the Alamo was airlifted to Las Vegas, Nevada where it now resides without complaint between the long legs of the Eiffel Tower.

The Perfume Wars

Speaking of Marseille, what came to be called "The Perfume Wars" was a snotty battle begun in Switzerland. "The Perfume Wars," of course, is the appellation Americans put upon themselves to pervade. The French Suisse, French Canadiens and French Côte d'Ivoirians told the Americans (in French) to put a lid on it—dubbing the combat "la guerre d'eau de toilette."

"The Perfume Wars" was a 3-year contest of indigenous noses that took face in June 2015. From Bogotá, Columbia where the South American winds blow; to Mokolodi, Botswana where the rhinos roam: All countries were game.

Top contenders were Switzerland's "Eau de Fromage"—concocted in the Gruyères, and the U.S.A.'s "Eau de Tuna"—created in Albacoreque, New Mexico.

To everyone's surprise, an underdog won the war: China's "Eau de la Foot," whose inventor said he knew his product was bound to win.

HEALTH AND EPIDEMICS

The Whore on Drugs

In the early 1900s, **Bertha Palmer**—wealthy socialite for whom Chicago's swanky Palmer House was built—invented the brownie by means of her chef. (He had money too.) Palmer was an esteemed, elegant woman.

But Palmer's reputation plummeted when—in 1905—word broke that she had posed for **Auguste Rodin**, sculptor of erotic poses. (Rodin's most controversial works: "The Eskimo Genital Kiss," "The Humping Dogs," and "The Bust of Bertie.") Although it wasn't given a head, "The Bust of Bertie" was voyeuristically reviewed as vulgar. The public figured out Bertha was the model the day she hid her head in shame when she guessed the public was about to figure her out.

Sensing Palmer's susceptibility, a jealous **Camille Claudel**—resentful that her lover Rodin didn't let *her* sculpt Palmer's bust—stirred cannabis into Palmer's Chamomile. Weak with rue, Palmer succumbed to infusions. Within a week, she was sprinkling cannabis on her crabs. Within a month, the dame was mixing marijuana into her brownies with the help of her chef. (He had attendants too.)

By 1907, Palmer was so strung out she fled to Mexico City via Nevada in her Tin Lizzie. She was *hungry*. She *needed bread*. Having thrown away her fortune—she drove about in fear and loafing for lost wages.

In Mexico City, fed up with food stamps that sullied her tongue, Palmer founded an institute of higher earning: a weed-garden bakery—christened "Potter's Panadería de Hierbajo." (She assumed her husband's forename **"Potter"** because it was just too perfect.) But in 1910 Mexican authorities arrested Palmer for potsitution.

Ninety-eight years later, POTUS Stewart called on Americans to pay respects to the founding mother of the brownie. Stewart, who appeared in the film "Half Baked" (1998), sympathized with the plight of the woman baker. (At first Americans were doobieous about their duty. But after a few deep breaths, they paid their tokings of respect.)

Palmer lived out her remaining years cramped in a cell in Cerro de los Guerreros (Warrior's Hill). Empathetically, Stewart drafted an extension of the medical use of marijuana to women suffering PMS—a measure spotted to take effect in 2018 on the 100th anniversary of Palmer's death.

The Regeneration of the Smartphone into the Human Hand

The first Smartphone "**Simon**" was introduced in 1992 by IBM (I Borrow Money). Twenty-three years later (2015), 91% of adult Americans have at least 1 Smartphone and 1 child named Simon. Now (2016), the average household has more Smartphones than smart people.

By 2010, Smartphones had become a fixture in human hands. By 2014, "users" became "abusers." By 2015, "abusers" became "addicts." Human hands that possessively clutched Smartphones—during sleep, herding sheep, etc.—evolved. Addicts' metacarpal anatomy began to mimic their owner's perpetual grip.

Hands transformed—curling as if cupping crests, thumbs aslope. Addicts were unfazed. In fact, their deformed hands made texting and emailing *easier*. Soon Smartphones started sticking to the flesh of palms and no longer needed charging. The devices mutated into living leech-like organisms—sucking static energy out of the addicts' skin cells to thrive.

Fingers fused into touchscreens. Knuckles kneaded into networks. Addicts could no longer pick up a fork without it dropping to the floor. How could they eat if they always knew someone was coming? Even worse, they *couldn't dial or type* without fingers! High fives hurt, and playing a game of "rock paper scissors" was just about impossible.

SAMHSA (Smartphone Abuse and Metal Hand Services Administration) drew a parallel and made a parable about the afflicted and **Tantalus**. Tantalus—a ravenous Greek God—was tortured in wrath by grapes dangling before him. The juicy fruit was almost…but not quite…in reach. SAMHSA went on to compare the afflicted to **Little Bunny Foo Foo**. Like Tantalus, Foo Foo was tortured by food dangling before him. In Foo Foo's case, it was carrots, not grapes. The carrots were a mere hop, skip, and a jump away…But Foo Foo was rooted in place, and could only follow the carrots with his eyes.

The worst cases (people who stare at their Smartphones while jaywalking, driving in farm-worker zones, nursing newborns, etc.) suffered "neck freeze." This is when the addict's neck stiffens while looking down—glazed eyes gazing at their screen. Their eyes function like gravitationally-sucked suction cups and *stick* to the screen—eyelids raised, eyes agape. The addict's cellular hands stick like superglue to his or her eyeballs—surfing in an un-blink-away-able glare.

The Fire Department Administration (FDA) tried to unstick the addicts' eyeballs from their screens by employing the frozen-tongue-stuck-to-the-pole treatment method. But pouring hot water into the victims' eyes only steamed their screens. Addicts steamed: How could they surf the web in water?!

Some addicts actually embraced their mutation. For example, cutting edge lovers had QR codes tattooed to their bodies so they could feel each other up.

In February 2016—just as addicts were finally getting a grip on their deformities—**Daniel Day Lewis** appeared in the new film "My Left Hand," portraying an afflicted Smartphone addict. Lewis's performance was so *brilliant*…so *poignant*…there wasn't a dry eye in the house. The movie-goers' buttery and salty tears short-circuited their cellular hands, which subsequently exploded. Shell-shocked addicts exited the cinema squinting—as if seeing the light of day for the very first time.

The healing addicts' human hands sprouted back—though forever slightly incurvated, cupping the air in withdrawal.

The Long Term Effects of Lasik Come to Light

In 2014, an unsightly scare scared scared Americans scared about the scare: On May 13 the nation—poised to ring in the 64th birthday of **Stevie Wonder**—witnessed a wondrous sight. Like any other May 13 sunset (8:14 pm D.C. time), the moon shone on the U.S.—but this eve its rays ricocheted off landlocked American borders. The moonshine staggered into Canadian and Mexican checkpoints, got turned away, and spun. In awe, the people beamed at the beams spinning and bouncing across this Land. (The Americans' diverted attention irked Wonder, who had always felt overshadowed by **Rays**.)

The next day, 8 million Americans awoke to an alarming spectacle: The white part of their eyes (scarera) had turned into stained glass! 16 million scareras were now mosaic-patterned—sprinkled with sensational shapes and shiny shades of color. Because their pupils were unaffected, the *people* affected could still see. However, most propped their eyelids up with toothpicks or cotton swabs in fear that blinking would shatter the glass and pierce their sight.

After a deep investigation conducted by Visual Spyes®, the public learned that stained glass scarera was a Lasik surgery-related reaction. Something about the moon's rays that May evening—cast upon Americans who used to lose and bump into things—turned cracked eye-whites into stained glass.

American Lasik under-goners—with the exception of ASASSSS (American Society of Apathetics, Self-Suppressors and Self-Sadists) members—rallied (having found new vigor) at the White House. Their reproach: America MUST find a cure or, at the very least, a Band-Aid approach that sticks. Millions shouted in unison, "I scream, you scream, we all scream for eye cream!"—over and over. Their voices got louder and louder. First soprano **Maria Aloysia Antonia Weber** chimed in with the same G6 she trilled in "Popoli di Tessaglia"—a concerto **Wolfgang Amadeus Mozart** wrote especially for her. The G6 was *so high* it shattered the stained glass in all 8 million Lasiked-Americans. Mosaic shards showered to their feet.

Victims screamed bloody murmur—until they saw their vision was still intact, their scareras again were white! Why, the mosaic had *not* been glass, but was rather harmless ceramic pieces of dried clay—crusty hardened residue that need only break to expose healthy, 20/20 eyes. Ophthalmologists resumed performing Lasik procedures, and pottery artists were staffed in the surgery rooms to save the clay.

AN ECONOMIC COLLAPSE AND ITS NIPPLE EFFECT

The Rise and Fall of the White Bread Factory: Cutting off the Trust

In Dec. 2007, Americans lost their grip when a recession pushed the country into a downward slide rail.

The recession was sparked by the collapse of Wells Fargo when Fargo kept falling down because it had too far to go. So Wells branched off to start the Wells Endowedment for the Arts. (Opening ceremony featured **Paul T. Anderson's** "Boogie Nights" on ride screen.)

All across the U.S. of A., hardworking slackers and slacking hard workers lost their jobs. Hundreds of thousands of people lost their livelihoods—due to mass layoffs by corporations such as Specific Motors (107,357), Ruralgroup (73,056), Merrill-Hug (40,650), and JP Morgan...Run! (22,852). Big box stores folded or went corrugated—sending ripples of disorder across America. The hardest hit were the white bread workers in Wheaton, IL.

The White Bread Factory, "Flavor Less Dough: Crust as You Like It®," in Wheaton was known for its—light, simple and practical—all-American product. In its heyday (November 30, 2007), Flavor Less Dough employed roughly 9,177,877 white bread workers in the State of Illinois. When the recession rained in (December 1, 2007), consumers stopped bringing home *any* kind of bread—even soggy. The bread makers were made rebundant and the factory closed.

At first the euphemistically-coined "bite-sized" rolled with it, but they soon realized man can only live by bread alone. It didn't matter how you sliced it; without bread, they were not men. **Melba Lara** of *WBEZ-Chicago* interviewed the bread worker emeriti. Their plea to the president: "Bail us out of this cr*p!" (rhymes with sap). Lara's microphone blew a fuse, and Americans who were paying attention heard: "Bail us out of this crop!" (rhymes with mop).

(Then) President Obama wasn't sure how to respond. So he decided to play it by ear—emptying out a bale of corn on a vacant lot. The laid-off bread makers assembled in a line, and waited their turn for their ration.

Obama-Éclair (The Affordable Heath-Bar Act) and the Smithsonian Sweet Tooth

On June 28, 2012, the U.S. Supreme Court held up a federal statue sculpted by (then) President Obama out of hard dark chocolate. The statue had been a monument of contention between liberals and conservatives since Obama carved it into law on March 23, 2010.

The law was technically titled "The Affordable Heath-Bar Act," but was nicknamed "Obama-Éclair" by the common man. The law obliged every U.S. business owner—with more than 49 personnel—to indulge each employee with complimentary chocolate bars and pastries. Owners who neglect to comp pie were to be assigned the toilsome task of injecting jelly into donuts and braiding lattice on pie tops.

Obama-Éclair also required Americans to buy chocolate bars and pastries for themselves and their families—thus ensuring adequate coverage for unexpected house calls and sleepovers. The law included a mandate that bulky Americans receive portions equal to those procured by the flimsy. "No body will be denied chocolate due to its weight!" Obama sang out.

Republicans were teething they were seething so much! They tried to rally dentist opposition to the Act® with Temptations But dentists didn't bite. (In fact, dentists forecasted the act reeling in some real revenue in fillings!) However, Republicans did win over *one* dentist-turned-public servant. Supreme Court Justice **Diana Floss** voted against Obama-Éclair. But Floss's vote was purely a symbolic gesture in a jealous stage against (60s girl group) **Candy and the Kisses.**

[In '81, Floss became the first woman justice appointed to the judicial branch. Before her appointment, the Supreme Court justices were suing the federal government to change their institution's appellation to: Steamy Court Racquetball of the United Men (SCROTUM). By the time their case made it to the Supreme Court, Floss had attained her seat. All it took was a little basic instinct and a leg lift "chair stare": Floss got all the balls in her court and the branch's name stayed set in stone.]

Three Years in the Running
Obama-Éclair launched October 1, 2013. It's been a rocky road, but today the act is widely savored. Business owners, in fact, quite *like* inducing chocolate lethargy in their employees. Trends demonstrate that today's employees fill up on free sweets and forgo lunch breaks—increasing their productivity due to sugar highs. And senior citizens are pleased that Medaéclaire provides them the plummest pickings in pastries at a reduced gait—and the unpopular Part D coverage gap (known as the "donut hole") will be closed by 2020.

Form and Sustenance
As a result of the highly flavorable Obama-Éclair, the human body evolved "Survival of the Unfittest" style. Women got loose and hippier. Men grew fleshy breasts—this enlarged their (now pancake-sized) nipples. Culture and technology evolved: "Social Media" switched into "Ice Cream Socials." The Internet inserted candy stripers into their URLs. Starbucks® swapped coffee with hot melted toffee. And…when Obama-Éclair mandated the lollypop replace the drumstick, Chick Filet® changed its name to Lick Filet® in expectation the peppermint would replace the patty.

The Smithsonian
Science and art metamorphosed with the rollout of Obama-Éclair. The Smithsonian was the first host of such realms to adapt. In the spring of 2015, the Smithsonian trumpeted its new revolutionary exhibit: "A Moveable Sweet." The tasteful exhibit—rumored to soon be made permanent—showcases a gallery of confections made ambulatory by demand. The apex of the exhibit is the *live demonstration of confectionary evolution*. Smithsonian scientists: 1. Slice gummy worms in half—both halves keep moving; and 2. Chop the heads off chocolate chickens—whose headless bodies run about in panic madly.

Part IV

THE PRESIDENTS PLAYHOUSE

The White House is a Fun House: From Remote Control Drones to "Being John Edwards"

After swearing into office, President Stewart married into a worldly country of astronomical debt. Economists attribute the nation's debt to two humiliating box office bombs:
1.) Democrats' poorly-made investment in the short-lived "Yes, We Can!" musical revue on ice.
2.) Republicans' poorly-made investment in the Fox Sci-Fi animated series: "Star Wars 84: Missile Defense Gone Ballistic."

With a deficit of more dollars than China has puppies (wagging and stewed), Stewart's political advisor **Axl Rose** advised drastic measures must be mistaken. Stewart retired to the Oval Office, put his feet up on his desk, and reclined back in his swivel chair. He placed his hands behind his head, and an arresting idea cuffed him:

"I will turn the White House into a Fun House!!! We'll demand a buck a head…or some doe if we charge the ladies. The Fun House's profits will pay off America's debt and accept charge cards so Americans can sink deeper into it!"

White House renovations went underway immediately, and the Fun House debuted in April 2015. Stewart established a senior committee to manage the Operation with tweezers. The committee went by the acronym "PAYTOPLAY" which stood for "Patriotic Americans Yearn To Operate Play-doh, Legos, And Yahtzee."

PAYTOPLAY stripped the lobby floors, replacing the marble with gymnastic mats. The committee painted the White House exterior with a fresh coat of bright white paint, and stuck glow-in-the-dark sticker stars on the interior ceilings for slumber parties.

In "The East Room," space was cleared for the Association of Hypnotists, Exorcists and Motivational-Speakers (AHEM) to provide some phonic relief. For *chronic* relief, "The Situation Room" was reserved for family interventions—citizens and permanent residents only. (At an extra cost, families can rent the Speaker of the House as mediator.)

The Fun House features:
- "Secret Service Segway Hunts" (SSSH)—staged tours to shoot mock assassins
- Mini remote control drones—"no fly zone" games for boys
- Bungee jumping from the debt ceiling
- Donkey and elephant rides
- The Dorian Gray Mirror Maze
- Foodcourt Exotica (seasonal)
- Bouncy castle (by reservation only, checkout's at noon)

President Stewart's brainchild was a prodigy! But not all the rides were propitious…

There was one *calamitous* attraction: the "Being **John Edwards**" ride. How it worked: Patrons crawled through a duct into a portal to Edwards' brain, and became him for an hour. When the ride was over, the patrons disembarked Edwards' brain feeling filthy and nauseous.

"It's, like, sickening," one pubescent patron was like, "I mean, it's like the President sicced [sic] a dirty jackass on my brain and called it industrious recreation" (SIC code: 7900).

The Stewart Administration shut down the ride—labeling it a mental health hazard.

The Presidents Playhouse: A Cellar Discovery

The Fun House beckoned buses of schoolchildren. Lines of kids littered the walk outside—waiting to be let in. On June 11, 2015, a 5-year old boy—in a winding, rollicking line—drew the plastic spoon from his cup of sherbet and commenced chipping at the foremost Fun House column. The column crumbled—like dried paper mâché—to reveal a fireman's pole leading underground. The pole was greased, a red stiletto wedged in the tall sheer metal rod.

The pole-leading-underground led to the disclosure of the BIGGEST classified cellar in U.S. history: The Presidents Playhouse.

That *not quite summer* day, the world learned that U.S. presidents have had a secret cellar since the White House was built in 1792. Only they, vice presidents, certain diplomats, select politicians, famous actors, and royal mistresses were granted access—pinky-sworn to secrecy.

Former President **John Adams**—the first president to reside in the new mansion—ordered the cellar built. Adams cited a need for privacy so he could compose the musical masterpiece "Nixon in China." (Some historians and musicologists theorize that Adams had the cellar built in an effort to feel "geographically closer" to China and to "better capture the Chinese essence" in his work.)

In 1920, the Presidents Playhouse opened a speakeasy: "The Draft Entry." "The Draft Entry" was accessible through a swing door bookshelf in the White House bomb shelter. The speakeasy's tagline: *Once You Enter the Draft, You Never Go Back.*

Other Presidents Playhouse amenities included "**Bill Clinton's** Cigar Bar"; **Spiro Agnew's** "Groovy Disco Dis Bar"; **Joe Biden's** "Biden Yer Time" relaxation spa; **Millard Fillmore's** library for young adult fiction; and the "The Happy and Gay Bipartisan Lounge." The latter featured a unisex restroom with writing on the walls that included "**Harvey Milk** was here (1977)" and "**Barbara Pierce Bush** was here, don't tell Dad (2003)."

Famished presidents and other sweet-toothed VIPs could frequent the CIA's French bakery "Treaties of Verspies," or indulge in a treat from a rusted vending machine—stocked with "The State of Maine Spruce Gum" (1848), "Squirrel Nut Zipper" (1905), "Goo Goo Clusters" (1913), "5th Avenue Candy Bar" (1936), and a "Whistle Pop" (1975).

The Playhouse is enormous. It's been hailed as "a village" and "rec room of the gods." The cellar—insulated with slabs of clay and cobble—has narrow paths and hallways lit with gas streetlamps.

The cellar stretches under pretty much the entire base of the White House. Dignified guests with weary legs could use **FDR's** wheelchair for smooth transit. And, as there were no ramps when the Playhouse was built, guests could use **Andrew Jackson's** hickory cane to descend *even further*—to reach the secret cellar's wine cellar where Adam's shovel lay to rest.

Now a Fun House highlight (open to the paying public), the Presidents Playhouse showcases dozens of relics and artifacts it accrued during—what has come to be known as—"The Secretive Years" (1792-2015).

Relics include: **JFK's** 45th birthday ice cream cake (sprinkled with frozen spittle); **Richard Nixon's** elongated wooden nose; **Bill Clinton's** elongated wooded sax; **Dan Quayle's** potatoe; **Abraham Lincoln's** applause; **Elvis Presley's** hotness; **Woodrow Wilson's** wife's uncast ballot; **Warren Harding's** poker face on china; **William Taft's** novelty t-shirt "I would gladly pay you Tuesday for a hamburger today"; **Ronald Reagan's** sweet tooth in a jar; the former Hexagon's missing wing; **Pablo Picasso's** *Harlequin Head*; **Andy Warhol's** can opener; **Stanley Kubrick's** *Eyes Wide Shut* chaise lounge; **Grover Cleveland's** bachelor party favors; **Teddy Roosevelt's** "Proud Union Home" yard sign; **Francois Mitterrand's** timeshare; **Michael Ducockpiss's** escape incontinent pet rooster; **Gerald Ford** and **Martin Van Buren's** 2-car garage; **Dennis Haysbert's** trailer; **King George VI's** teleprompter; and Stewart's own contribution: a bar of soap for washed out mouths.

Life after Laughs

Regrettably, the Stewart term is up this year. Pee-Yew Research Center (PYRC) reports a majority of Americans expect Stewart will run for a second term. We can hope, but only Late Night can substantiate the speculation.

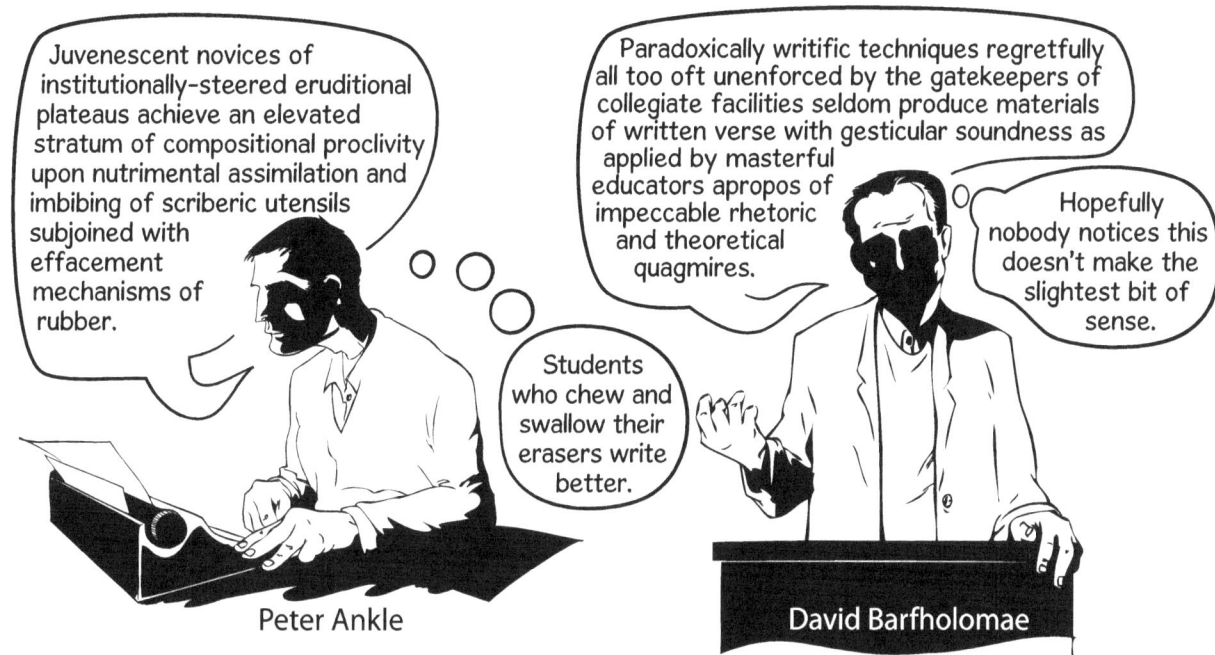

ENGLISH COMPOSITON

PETER ANKLE

Edifying the Heads of the Student Body by Means of Application
of the Romance Languages as a Didactic Discipline of the Composition of the English Tongue

In the most fecundest of cognizant theories of scribe, the most feckless of notions doth be that English composition best be-ith taught in the English lexicon. In my palpable brilliancy, I argue that such a practice is pure palaver. The puissantest methodology of English composition pedagogy lays in the manuscription and complementary catechetical instruction of the Romance languages.

Now, the Romance vernacular encompasses the holistic span of such slopes and curvatures in Western European dialect—sans English—that birthed the English language with which to begin. The Romance patois is not unlike the sweeping thoroughfare of cobbled stones in ancient Catalonia, fresh and invigorative post hoc its street cleaning the tertiary Sunday of the month. It is also not unlike the Cyclopean chasm of the Verdon Gorge in contemporaneous France, aloft cruise dauntless zipliners to-and-fro, as airborne as the accents grave ` and aigu ´.

In order for a feeble, ineruditial pupil to judiciously indict English prose and poetricular balladry, the youthful or returning pupil must firmly grasp the alphabetical notes and nuances of those amorous modi operandi of verbal exchange. Ensuing mastery of the romantic mouth, cometh the hour for the apprentice of wisdom to put her head down and seize the pen with quill. Should the scholar-in-waiting possess an encephalon as blank as the paper upon which ink must leak, is this a call for admonishment and defeat? Is this a decree of scandal and chastisation? I argue no; for the dense learner-at-heart is merely wading into step 1 of **free association**, which occurs when the student doeth relate her blank mind to the page. Step 2 then pursues; the association of the liberated metamorphasizes into **free writing**, i.e., a technique upon which the statutes of grammar and expository skill do not pertain. [1]

As I charmingly profess in *Writing with Flour,* my essayic masterépicerie, my dissertational cream of the crop, so to speak, free writing is like pie: evenly dividable into two pieces, both of which students must swallow for just attainment of a ceremonious graduation. Yes, that pinnacle of existence-justification. It may sound toilsome to digest should the student's tooth reject its sweet cream; however, I argue the imperativeness that the student choke down my vapid logic which furnishes the expressly clever theory that one slice of the pie is **criterion-based**, and the approximal slice is **reader-based.**

Now, in the context of my proclamation that the most efficacious method of nurturing the craft of English composition is by means of imbibing the languages of the Romantics. Now, should I stray from this theorem, I must remind myself ofttimes, that in order to excel as the captain, if you will, of the vessel of English composition theory, I must veer straight ahead with affected conviction that my novel ideas are radical and revolutionary. Thus:

Free writing is, literally, writing without thinking. While such a feat may seem preposterous to most academics or mortals with an IQ of over 20, I'm of the rare breed that embraces asininity with not just open arms, but with open legs to boot. Now, the criterion-based technique poses upon the utterly inept, aspiring writer the need to heed quality of content of the meager work at hand. Now, should the examined party undertake this drill in English, consider the intrinsic barriers that hinder realization of an astute analysis of caliber writing. Now, why would a student examine their free-writingly composed paper, only to attempt reassess its value? It's illogical. Now, granted I devised the concept to begin with, but one may call oneself a superior scholar when they are humbly able to refute their own theories for the purpose of having something to say.

Yes, inherently tenured professors and emeriti may hem and haw over the lack of the students' progression or, in some unfortunate cases, even their accelerated decline attributable to pupils' vexation at the futility of writing and rewriting the same thing with the same 171,476 words in the English dictionary. Tedious! I do not cast blame upon these souls made hopeless by the confines of their institution, and their alleged "department" of English. "Compartment" is more actual! Locked inside a stuffy, musty language that hails from Teutons and colloquial British Commonwealth. However, if an instructor applies an ebb and flow of a Romance language—*whichever* you choose- French, Spanish, Portuguese, Italian, Walloon, what have you—the melodic dialect continuum [for all Romance languages are in cursive] transmits from your frenetic brain to your mouthoral womb down your residual throat trickling down either arm—contingent upon your left or right-handedness—simultaneously through your thumb and index, and finally flooding down through the pen to its tip, ejaculating ink onto page. One cannot achieve such cuneiform bliss in the frigid confines of English. No, one needs the fire and passion of "Besarte es como ver las estrellas" ; "Sei il mio universo"; "Voulez-vous coucher avec moi?" to craft the English phrases "Kissing you is like inserting stars into my eyes"; "You are as big as the universe to me"; "Won't you come to bed now, Dear?" with eloquence.

And now let us steer our maiden ship into the second piece of pie: the reader-based technique of English composition. Reader-based composition method means the writer asks oneself, "Why did I write this really?" and "What value has it, if any?" Reader-based processes commit a mental processing of imagery and dramatic reenactment of the free-written piece. [2] So, let us survey this: In the English language, if the student thinks in their native tongue (or English if they're Hispanic) and jots down the stale, concrete words as they exist motionless in their mind, what imagery does that evoke? Cold. Institutional. Compartmentalized. How thrilling is the dramatic reenactment of the "script"? Monotone. Inconsequential. Trite. So, let us now weave our newfound knowledge into this perplexing equation. Consider: Should we integrate a *variety* of Romance languages into the work, consider the spirited imagery and conceptualization of the process that will arise. "¿Puedo llevar puesto su stilettos?"; "Posso sentire il tuo profumo?"; "Enlevez vos vêtements, vous nymphomane!" Now doesn't this add flare to your English expressions: "May I try on your heels?"; "You smell like a possum without a tail"; and "Let's play spin the bottle, Cutie!"

A copycat of my masterful theory, Patricia Gizzard of the College of the Bowl in Sauce in Worcester, MA, attempted to introduce a third slice in a fruitless effort to snatch a piece of my pie. The silly boob definitively stated that there is a third slice of pie to complement criterion-based and reader-based. Gizzard introduces a vacuous technique she coined **butter-based**. In Gizzard's theory, the collegiate pupil learns English composition on a slippery slope, laden with fat from too much sedentary reclinement. Now if I were to buy into her rudimentary theory, of which I clearly never shall, in line with my proclamation of the Romance languages, I would better associate the pie with a hornazo, which is a tasty Spanish meat pie of chorizo and loin. As opposed to Gizzard's asinine analogy—equating rhetorical theory to a buttery, flakey "All American" apple pie. Concisely put: America and Great Britain have no place in the English language. Strip yourself of this biased phantasm.

Now, if I may segue: A tip to the wise "wanna-be's," to put it crudely. If you, the reader—who is, presumably, a *longing-to-be-deemed-as-esteemed* professor or a greatly misled graduate student of English pedagogy—buy into my Bolognese argument, then I advise you to arm yourself with an electronic urban dictionary that translates any given language at any given time. Despite, in this questionable modern age with questionable youth well-versed in technology, that such an electronic gadget is likely bugged or "hot." Keep tight in skull the wise words of Lennon, "Happiness is a warm tongue"[3] to guide you. In the classroom (your one-man theatre, if you will), your disciples will attempt to partake in covert communication channels in an imprudent, insolent lingo with the intention of instilling upon the instructor receptivity of isolation, insecurity of dotardidly aging, and fear of campus gangs. Thus you must elevate your skull, and enter thy class armed with your electronic pocket translator. Poise yourself to pull the trigger whenst a foreign word sonically arise. Marvelous ammunition! The wonderful thing about triggers is triggers are a wonderful ping. "I'll ping you later," I oft hear over my students parlaying. If you cannot beat them, whip them by mastering their cellphonic dialect. This will impress upon them the genius of those with matter caged within skulls.

Now, returning to the intended discourse, I dare say it should *not* be an expectation for the teacher to cognitively acquire the languages of the Romantics in order to *teach* English composition. [4] Thus the students shall best master the key, commonmost-contemporarily-practiced Romantic languages—those being naturally French, Spanish, and Italian. (Unless, of course, the student aims to enroll in "Pointless Lit" - LAE 789; in which case she should master the *obscure* Romance languages like Friulian and Leonese.) Following the students' completions of these Romance language courses, the ever-so-slightly more highly educated pupils may progress to English Composition 101. Devil's advocates may argue: How can a professor teach English through the application of the Romance Languages when he doeth be merely unilingual. These devilish shortsightenders will attempt the debate: If the English teacher does not, in the voluptuous verse of Madonna, "Practice what you preach," who or what guides the impressionable youth?

Musingly, I keenly identified an almost plausible answer: College students so oft be stoned, thus they should have no problem reading Rosetta.

As with any stroke of geniusortal supremacy, the professorial Deity will have its trifling adversaries, its King Herods, its challengers in the ring centered within slews of empty, tiered bleachers. While the name does'nth spring naturally to mind, upon tapping into that memory chunk of the cerebellum that deposits the meaningless, easily forgettable facts and silly untruths, a David Barfholomae makes his presence known. An ill-regarded self-proclaimed theorist of English composition, Barfholomae publically challenged my erudite declaration of the chicken and the egg theory. I am confident that the writer exists in the egg without grooming, while Barfholomae argues the writer is the chicken. [5]

Ample shenanigans they be, and so moveth we at this time forth unto reason. Let us reflect upon semantics. "Romance" is derived from the Vulgar Latin term "romanice." At the time (27 BC), civilized villagers presumed the Roman Empire was simply trying to get their citizens to like them. "English" back when it was Old (5th Century), is the language of Anglo-Saxons, a peoples of medieval character, frequently out. The Romancers utter an amalgamation of tenses and moods, passions like wildfire spewing spittle; whilst the Englishers shoot simplicity in a phlegmatic, analytical Germanic goober. What ties the disparate languages in ensemble is their mighty mother, known by most as Indo-European tarp under which all child languages cower.

I was a mere adolescent when I composed my first book, *Writing Without Bleachers*. Within I examine my teen choice to take to pen in high school and waive jocular sports like pubescent courting and playing ball. Even then, as I rolled my pen in waves—tide rushes in, tide rushes out—I felt romance run through me, and yet my words were of English descent and on paper, bitty blots. But I knew at that time now that I look back at it in an effort to draw a parallel, that the Romance languages were channeling through me and manifesting themselves in brilliant English script.

And so followeth my second masterful production, *Believing in Q-Bert* attribute my adeptness at English gaming, published by Gottlieb, an entity of Germanic origin, and when looking back, I see now—because it conveniences me—that when I deconstructed Q-Bert's language, its isometricity evenly divided into cubes of equal proportion, that could be decoded into secret English messages. Messages like "If you call them, they will come probably," and "He who shall not be named shall be named." In hindsight, the influence of Romance language into my mechanical, linguistic analysis played a large part in my ability to write this work. My analysis: listening in heavy headsets to "Games without Frontiers" by pop artist, Peter Gabriel [6] in which he sings "Jeux sans frontieres" in torturous repetition.

I clearly dove subliminally headfirst into learning and now teaching English Composition with ghost of a romantic. In fact, at one time I aspired to be a ghost writer. I don't buy into ghosts, but I do believe in life after words. Yes, I've been reckless; my tenure not without controversy, my ideas not without argument. I have founded new courses such as "Artistic Liberty and Creative Writing for Court Reporters," and "Philosophy of Improvisational Teaching" which is an avant-garde method in which an English teacher prepares nothing. [7] Yes, Sir, I've caused a stir in my time. Indeed, I've been known to lift my skirt and show some ankle!

Now to conclude, I will give this literary jewel a peruse—in true reader-based spirit! Hmm, ah yes, very nice! I must fess up; I'm delightfully pleased, amassed with splendid self-pride, that I've wrapped this up in Week 1. Now I am free to spend the next ten months of my sabbatical in Bermuda. Amen for Academia.

My brilliant career it is, to state in 97 sentences what a mere schoolchild could state in one.

References
[1] Ankle, P. "The Uses of Binary Fingers," *Journal of Advanced Composition* (1993)
[2] Ankle, P. "The Music of Porn," *College Composition and Communication* (2006)
[3] Lennon, J. "The White Alum," Produced: English Matriculating Interns (EMI) (1968)
[4] Ankle, P. "Coming to Manhood as a Vernacular Intellectual" *College Composition and Communication* (2008)
[5] Ankle, P. with Barfholomae, D. "Responses to the Egg and Chicken Debate" *College Composition and Communication* (1995)
[6] Gabriel, P. "(Self-Titled)" Produced: Lillywhite, S. (1980)
[7] Ankle, P. "Should We Invite Students into Our Homes? Complicating the Yes/No Debate" *Composition Studies* (2007)

RHETORICAL THEORY

DAVID BARFHOLOMAE

Extrapolating the Fundamentals of Dexterous English Composition By Tutelagical Virtue, Endemic to Asian Languages and Chinese Symbolism

One dismal morn, the fabricated heavens as gray as brain matter, I had the grave misfortune to stumble upon an Ankle in the latest *Composition Forum*. I had browsed Peter Ankle before, including the essay we co-authored "Responses to the Chicken and Egg Debate," although I never could—nor will—digest his preposterous theories of English instruction and correlating undergraduate absorption. Ankle's latest monstrosity, "Ingesting the Heads of the Student Body by Means of Asphyxiation of the Romance Languages," is ignoble and witless. I heed its readers to arm yourselves with my very essay at hand to shield your pitiable minds from pivotal risk of further deterioration and schizophrenia. [1]

I recap in the most non-offensive way possible, an exacting exploit: Ankle senselessly purports that the most efficacious approach to fruitful teaching of English composition is by expectation the student must become astute in Romance languages should she wish to possess talent and progress in her English writing endeavors. Such conceit, Ankle! To assume that a student should veritably acquire fluency in Romance languages which are vernacular instruments within the Latin alphabet when English *itself* is an apparatus of that very same alphabet! (Ankle attempts to justify this by clarifying: "Romance is derived from Vulgar Latin." Vulgar, indeed!) How is this, to quote Ankle's infantile work—about as meticulous as a toddler's finger painting—"reckless" and "avant-garde?" More befitting characterizations would be "prosaic" and "antiquated."

Ankle's self-proclaimed self-formulated theory is *not* based in original thought, but any half-witted Ivy League Ph.D. would be aware that the Roman Language studential instillment method of eruditional deployment dates back to 1925 with the coming of Lawrence A. Cretin who went on to profess anti-intellectual theory at Columbia University, S.A. Cretin was the first to assert that a college pupil's assimilation of French and Italian (Spanish in that era was not yet a ubiquity) nourished the learner's cognitive capability to produce creative conceptualizations and compose quality papers in English. [2] Even decades later, James Berlint, a rhetorical theorist who advocated the integration of communist theories into contemporary English compositions, tendered a similar prosody. In his book "The Politics of Histrionicgraphy," Berlint hints at, of all things, the ineffectiveness of melodramatic Romance languages as a tool of English composition in his therein statement, "I will not subscribe to a Utopia until all Latin language writings are translated into the Cyrillic alphabet or shredded. Withal this; kindly shred upon completion of my epilogue." [3] I rest my case and chortle!

Alleged academics in the esteemed cosmos of English Rhetoric need reassess their integrity when questioned. I, and indubitably others of post-pubescent masterly mind, question Ankle, who clearly, judging by the inarguable decline of his—now whimsical—works, is petering out. He has become, if you will, a storm chaser. The reader surely knows the anthropological demographic: a deluded, self-aggrandizing climatologist starved for attention who throws himself into a twister to make the evening news and to appear indispensable to his employer. In English theory academia, Ankle is, what I have cleverly coined, a *brainstorm* chaser! As substantiated by my references to Cretin, Berlint and Barfholomae, it is evident that Ankle's daily ablutions consist of reading compositional theory cliff notes; exhuming ideas of incapacitated rhetoricians; claiming precocious graduate students' papers as his own; and inviting himself into Circle Time at the Avery Coonley School for Gifted Children.

Indeed, Ankle plops down all fours, cuspidated nose thrust to the floor, skittering about sniffing, chasing and sucking "thought" mites up through his nose, a vernacular vaccuum (!)—its little trivial ideas or variations of the ratherly more fertile ideas of others—flitting about like circus fleas caged in the dust bag, his unfiltered brain turning tricks with all the dignity of a dancing bear. Once he assimilates the mites and lines his fleas up in a row, he spews forth an obtuse conclusion, squirting ill-conceived and plagiarized thought-balloons in duos out his nostrils: yanking them down by the strings, coveting them, blowing them up tighter with hot air 'til they pinch, and publishing them as his own.

Now, I am intimately acquainted with the creative process and the electrochemical process with its neurotransmitters inseminating vacuousness via penetration of the synaptic gap. In Ankle's case, the creative neuroscientific process consists of scrofulous dirty little secrets that Ankle has poached and assorted into an offensive concoction upon which he micturates and soils.

Be wary: A storm chaser invariably travels with a camera crew on call. Heed caution, bleary reader; despite the lusting lineup to fill the vacancies, do not commit yourself to Ankle's crew. For, should you band with his slothy minions, he will spellbind, misguide, and invoke in you inextinguishable self-immolation.

And now that I have keenly refuted Ankle's dastardly conjecture that the integration of the Romance languages in English composition (ridiculous!) improves the undergraduate writing experience; prepare yourself, readers, to be astounded, mandibles agape. For I am about to break wind of a gargantuan, potent revelation; a gale that will bowl readers over in incredulity: **The application of Orient languages as the edificational mechanism to which a college student must operate in order to excel in the discipline of English composition.**

Now observe; I am not speaking of the trite Indo-European languages which include Hindi, Russian, Armenian, and those prima-donnaesque Romance languages. I am talking about bona fide calligraphic Asian bodies: Seno-Tibetan, Altaic, Mon–Khmer, and Tai-Kadai. When contemplating Orient alphabets, the image that springs to mind is symbols, which are small pictures or graphics that show you what you want to hear. For example, "你是驚人的" means "You are breathtaking" in Chinese (Sino-Tibetan). "ฉันสามารถนอนหลับมากกว่า" means "Can I sleep over?" in Thai (Tai-Kadai). "이 아이스크림 저지방입니다" means "This ice cream is low fat" in Korean (Altaic). And "តើខ្ញុំគួររង់ចាំបីថ្ងៃដើម្បីហៅទូរស័ព្ទទៅនាង?" means "Should I wait three days to call her?" in Khmer (Mon-Khmer).

Oh, those lines: sloping, crisscrossing, slippery, scrawl childlike—rich with poignancy and enlightenment; its pleasing scribbles piquing our interest like peaks of Mount Fuji, its pictorial jagged blots glistening like the tips of barbed wire atop the Great Wall on a sunny day. Oh language, unfurl your innocent Asian tongue or let me curl up into its decadence.

For those privileged pupils who have succeeded in testing or nosing their way into my courses at University of Armpittsburg, PA, good fortune has rained upon you niblets of my genius. In all your ignorance, your dozens of spirited little legs skitter up to my lectern with outstretched bony arms, phalanges grasping at my kernels of wisdom like parade- spectating kids at candy. Indeed, for years I have preached the universality of symbolic application as the catalyst for proficient, generative writing as a method. Have I not Socratically-projected upon you, my students, these questions feigned as rhetorical?

- π   What is English Comp if not the Cambodian Slip of the Tongue?
- π   What is English Poetry if not the Manchu Meter of Matriculation?
- π   What is English Literature is not the Laotian Lyre of the Lesson?
- π   What is English Creative Writing if not the Burmese War of the Words?

It is imperative to retain: There are few brilliant worldly professors and theorists (e.g., Einstein, Hawking, Sacks, Barfholomae) whose God-assigned task is to walk the earth without mankind's input. However, for the lower "lifes," (i.e., the vast populous) collaborative group classwork is necessary in order to shake up the coins in the collective pot. Consider: if each student's brain contains one cell of wisdom, mix it with the other one cell of another student's wisdom, and, if you are a group of seven, you are six cells smarter than when you started. It's an old ideological— albeit it idiotic—idiom, but as the Chinese say, there's no "我" in "Team." ⁽⁴⁾

Reader, I implore you to grasp: There is no "man." There is no "woman." We are all our own unique selves; we are all our own unique genders, with our unique voices on paper—7.1 billion of which, to be exact. (Voices, not paper.) And thus, appreciate our differences but integrate with our own kind. (Get it? Asian syllabary= difference /& alphabetical integration=English semantics!) Yes, it may sound paradoxical, but Doctors support there can be great joy to mingle with students of the opposite sex of the same caliber. In other words, if you cannot "do it right," don't "do it alone." The first country to ascertain and abide by this instructional mantra was, that's correct, China with its 1.4 billion voices.

我 told you so!

I instruct my students to "take your seat and reflect upon your pen. For you must take pen in order to take flight." And in order to genuinely experience the Asian languages firsthand in their *authentic* environment, taking a flight is *exactly* what you must do. Ankle blathers that the American student may take continental flight in order to excel (e.g., pop over to Quebec or take a hop, skip, and a thump to Cancun) in English comp. But studying domestically/continentally is not a deep enough dive to tap into the brain's Broca and the Wernicke to process grammar and syntax and produce English composition. By exercising your polyglottal abilities in your brain's anterior cingulate whilst the curvatures and hieroglyphic flare provide the student with a limber, nimble nervous system better capable of formulating thoughts eloquently on paper.

Now, let us regard—repellent though be it, at Ankle's *Romance Languages* essay. Within this "work" Ankle attempts to dissect composition into two categories; combined he crudely refers to as "a pie." The first category he tags "criterion-based" which he argues helps the writer question their own writing during the writing process. Silliness indeed. Everyone knows that a writer must question her work BEFORE commencing the writing process. How can a professor feel superior if the student enters the process with confidence and enthusiasm? Secondly, Ankle calls the second category "reader-based" which is, according to this dimwitted dimwit, a state of mind in which the writer pictures the story as the reader sees it. This is especially silly; since the writer reads her own work, why would she make the effort to mentally project to herself what she is already envisioning which in turn becomes an endless exchange of duplicated thoughts in incessant repetition which would clearly drive her mad! So to Ankle's "pie" I say, "Criterion-based, my foot!" "Reader-based, my elbow!" "Hogwash-based" is more like it!

Clearly, passion for studential writing maturation is not Ankle's driving force. Certainly, he wades in the waves' white tips of pedagogically comped-application, but only up to his ankle. For to Ankle, it is purely *ego* and *appetite*. (Perhaps his next book should be titled *I Am Hungry For Myself.*) When Ankle should be pontificating about pedagogy, he's pontificating about pie! When he should be pulpiteering composition, he's pulpiteering chorizo! [5] Well, the average numbskull may interpret Ankle's consumption obsession as a sign of cibarious hunger; however, the truth is Ankle is FULL of it; the only body part of his that's devoid is the hole between his ears. And yet, despite his fixation of foods and likeability, his theories are highly unpalatable and pretentious. I garner he fancies himself Gruyère, but in actuality he's Velveeta—flimsy and processed. Or perhaps not, since he doesn't seem to process much in the ole' attic. Come to think of it, his pouting theories are mild in flavor and abundant with holes; he must be Baby Swiss! Whatever the cheese, I—and indubitably countless others—am of absolute resound that Ankle is no Gouda! (Gouda joke © 2013 Barfholomae, D.)

While on the subject of sustenance—both intellectual and abdominal—Ankle absurdly cites our co-authored work and embarrassing (for him) "agreement to disagree" on the Chicken and Egg debate. It's frankly nothing short of imbecilic that Ankle claims the egg must be warmed and stroked in order to nurture the unborn writer. Hodge Podge, Sasquatch! It's clear as clarity, that the writer is the CHICKEN, and must be called as such to progress and hone her skills. No matter how aggressively I hammered this realism into Ankle's noggin, he just kept on blowing hot air, sticking to his gums. In our essay "Responses to the Chicken and Egg Debate," Ankle writes, "I respect Dr. Barfholomae, but frankly, I don't relish his chicken theory. He keeps beating everybody over the head with the respective fowl." Well, Ankle, coming from you that's a condiment! Foul indeed! Perhaps he'd swallow it easier with an injected IV feeding him liquid Egg McMuffins in his veins given his obsession with those cracked shelled ovals and their fetal yolks.

Another bone I have to pick with Ankle is his analogy of language *acquisition* and cooking *application*. In his (2005) essay "How to Enhance Yearning by Using Pork-Stakes and Beef-Stakes in Writing" he claims pork-bellies are to beef patties like making-love-to-language-orally is to a roll in the hay—Citing they are just as tasty without the buns. Now, there is no meat to this ludicrous parallel. [6] Oh my, his piteous pupils, whose fathers actually *pay* for this abhorrent instruction. His pupils may as well be tending their papers by eraser not lead. I implore Ankle's students: Pay no attention to the man behind that lectern, or better put: Pay no attention to the man behind that apron. He never stops speaking, and yet not one plausible thought evacuates his mouth.

His notion of pedagogy is as trite as a "pedi-mani" except he's not a man in my eyes, so why is he painting his feet? What is that he says about…oh yes, Ankle writes "I am free to spend the next ten months of my sabbatical in Bermuda." Bermuda Triangle is more like it! When I take sabbaticals I buckle down for a solid year, only taking Sundays off for service. I expect when Ankle returns from the Bermuda Triangle he'll fancy his next sabbatical be in Palm Springs to encourage Montessori schoolgirls to run wild. While my theories are interior, evolved, and as industrially complex as North Korea, Ankle's are as simplistic and repetitive as the Wheels on the Bus.

Many an eve have I silently expounded on my pillow upon the arguments that arise against my theory. While I don't entertain them for long, they help me fall asleep. Now one eve a mere fortnight ago, I was feeling adventuresome and so I opted for a mug of Vinacafe, a Vietnamese brand of coffee, in place of my usual light-roast Eight O'Clock Coffee after dinner at four. The Vinacafe's tagline is "Hương vị của thiên nhiên" directly translated: *The Taste of Nature*. I inserted a striped stir-stick skinny straw into the infusion, the instant granular copper-glazed bits appeared as innocuous as Dunkin. [7] And then I sucked. Blistering java erupted from my mouth like lava from the Haut Dong Nai. Nature indeed! The scorching brassy muck oozed forth from my oral trench, through my teeth, over my lower lips, and down my chin. I called on my wife to dredge my mouth for sores and weeds.

The epiphany I experienced at that moment was fantastical. Conventional wisdom propounds: "In order to write, one must read. In order to read, one must speak. In order to write well, one must read well. In order to read well, one must speak well." Well, what if one *couldn't* speak well? Conventional wisdom, that icy swan, claims that that speaker therefore must be ill at scribe. And yet, as my mouth burned from scalding alkaloidic shrubbery, I was capable of grasping pen and writing—in the leather journal my wife fetched—my **most fetching work of revelational theory** as it pertains to epistemological evolution of the didactic method for articulating the genesis of all scholarly theories of higher educational institutions**:… (Drum roll)… My revelation (!):** In order for the student to write well, the student <u>MUST</u> <u>BE</u> <u>AWAKE</u>. Ahhh! My radical discovery! My contribution to academic society! This, most certainly, is what I'll go down for!

And so, an adversary may argue—and has—that I am downright biased toward the Asian argot, given its purgative endowment of my vowels and cathartic influence on my bowels. These claims may contain grains of truths; nevertheless, I embrace my quixotism, and stand unwavering at the illusory Pacific shore, waving to the imaginary immigrants debarking, unclasping their billions of suitcases on the dock releasing a trillion hieroglyphic symbols into the sky. I figuratively intake their oriental loops, swallow their slashes, swish their swirlys around my scarred mouth, imbibe their pointless arrows; drinking all the letters of their alphabets in like flights of bubbly. **And I am a better writer for it.**

Now, you can tell by the way that I use my balk; I'm an important man with no time to small-talk. I'm extraordinarily busy and demanded, and so I will leave you with this:

Class dismissed. Away with you.

References

[1] Barfholomae, D., Ph.D., "Extrapolating the Fundamentals of Dexterous English Composition By Tutelagical Virtue, Endemic to Asian Languages and Chinese Symbolism," *Self-Published*
[2] Cretin, L., "American Education: An Extensive Look at Centuries of National Experience, 1783-1784," *Harper and Row*
[3] Berlint, J., "There's No Business Like Know Business," *Playbill*
[4] 未知，" 這是一個狗吃狗的世界。" " 中國青少年雜誌 "
[5] Ankle, P.U., B.A., "Ingesting the Heads of the Student Body by Means of Asphyxiation of the Romance Languages," [Page 2, Peepee. 3] *Composition Snoreum*
[6] Barfholomae, D., Ph.D., "Writing on the Margarine: A Composition Cookbook" *Bedrest Books*
[7] Dunkin, R. "Falling Head Over Heels: My Mentorship of Humpty Davy, the Founder of the Science of Electrochemistry," *The Barometer*

An excerpt from Anne Lamott Applesauce's *Tail by Tail: Some Instructions on Writing and Vibes*

Bad Ass Drafts

Now, pretty much all good writers write drafts. Some write two drafts, some write twelve drafts. Some write drafts while drinking draft. Some write drafts in the breeze. Stupid writers write daft because either the r key is broken or they don't know how to spell.

Now, people who don't write or who haven't read my book are stupid too. People have a worldwide misperception that good writers perch on their desks every morning, feeling like a million bucks, a great story about to spew forth onto the blank coveted sheet, release a few deep blasts of gas, give themselves a slap on the ass and dive in.

The truth is that good writers are not happy. Even those who are published or rich, scratch their scalps writing. Good writers are miserable and wish that they made their fortune publishing cookies. Good writers are not drenched in dew, bouncing about like huskies on trampolines. They are dictators. (My pagan friend Tom says you can safely say you are writing in God's image when you know your friends hate you.)

Now, for me, writing is exasperating. In fact, the only way I can get anything written is to write really, really, really, really, really bad ass drafts.

Knowing your draft will be for your eyes only, you may swagger your fingers between the words and upend their sweet chastity. There's a bad boy inside everyone chomping at your spit to get out. Now, for a writer to write that one beautiful line, they will release the bad boy from their mouths to romp all over your ink.

If one of your characters wants to say, "Well, so what, Miss Snoopy Pants?," let your bad ass express himself. If you want to write nasty, harassing stuff like: "This is a stick up. I'm armed. Act normal. Put cash in bag. Singles too," or like, "All work and no play make Jack a dull boy," then write it.

Now, if there is a line that leaps out at you as a winner, a true piece of quality writing, mark it with an asterisk, so that when you are at page bottom, you will have the flexibility to shake up your abundant body of words, and tighten them later. Don't be bummed if you don't nail it the first time. You can bet your bottom dollar it will come back to you, and you'll be swimming in booty like me.

I used to write food reviews for California's *LA Youth* magazine, before it folded due to my lame ass jokes about purée and peacock brains. ("Their mushy brain is in their bottom," I joked.) I was really good at writing food reviews because I researched restaurants and ate their food. It took me two days to write about each meal because I'm slow to digest.

It didn't matter if I was reviewing a formal eatery or a food cart. At first I would always panic. How am I going to capture the essence of the wiener before it went down? Before it went through? Before it went out? In the end, it always worked out. But not without the bad ass draft.

When I took the first stab at writing a review with taste, the result was nauseating. The review was so flavorless it may as well have been cream of corn. I taught myself to put my good girl away, unbutton my blouse to the bottom of my sternum, and show a little rib. At my desk I'd spike my shrub with brandy, and sprinkle my cornflakes with grated hemp.

I'd type up invitations, challenging other writers to drag-race with me and play Russian roulette. I stopped combing my hair, and let my dreads spill down into the shrub below. The words flowed, they were cheeky and asinine. I'd make cracks about inappropriate subjects like shooting up and Charles Manson. I'd write swear words. I'd write threats. I'd write dirty limericks. I'd write innuendos. I'd write graffiti. I'd write rap lyrics.

Do you know what? Don't answer, I'll tell you: It worked.

After releasing my bad boy on paper, I was able to take a break to collect myself and shower. Then, after some cold Chow Mein, I returned to my draft and cleaned it up. My writing was now pristine and prudish. Potent, but still virginal. My innocent rewrites are masterpieces. One story at a time, tale by tale.

Ever since my bad ass discovery, I have been exercising this writing technique on my drafts. I like to see hypnotists to help me exorcize my demons when it's time to convert my potty mouth to prissy. My nice hypnotist is intrigued by me. He gave me this exercise to do because he thinks I'm fascinatingly complex:

Close your eyes and shut up. Listen to the voices in your head. Listen to the voices as if they are scurrying around on your head in a million directions. They are the voices of your high maintenance parents who bore ungrateful children; they are the voices of your colleagues nagging at you the same way you nag at them; they are the voices of your children happily playing.

Imagine these irritating voices are lice, and you pick them up one by one by the tips of their tiny anal plates, and plop them into a mason jar. When you have filled the jar with all the tiny lice, turn up your head volume and listen to their voices blasting. Then, lower the volume all the way down, so that you have muted all the people's voices so you can get back to your draft.

One friend of mine suggests beheading the lice on a chopping block. But I'm sure nothing like this would occur to you. *(Wink Wink.)*

Now, like this essay. No one is going to read this bad ass draft unless it's printed by error in place of my refined essay Random House accepted for publishing. So, I can write anything I want. Like: Piss off readers! I am Goddess of the Pen! *Tail by Tail* will be a best seller! *The Seattle Times* will call it "A gift to all of us mortals." I am Anne, Anne-I-Am, and I do so like green eggs and spam. I am drenched in dew! I am happy!

Make No Room for Kids: Bells Ding for Online Classes K-8
An Argumentative Abstract by Richard Fukerson
Sponsored by The University of Phonics

Any pedagogical theory, irregardless of its self-aggrandizing maker, that enlists the nerve to counter the ground breaking, earth shattering eruditional philosophy about to be put forth, is by any definition, a vainglorious, foolhardy soul, forever lost in the woods of antiquated methods and prehistoric deliverance.

My lengthy, long-winding path of research, dating back to my childhood composition studies at the playground for precocious tots—whereon I conjugalmated verbs with mothers on chalk—to my locker room argotic antics at the junior school of higher education wherein I swept my finger on shower doors punctuating steam—my portfolii of reconnoitering writifical exploration qualifies me to proclaim the following findings a truth: worthy of regulatory application and subsequent penalization for neglect to comply.

The very nature of my familiarity with youthful scribe commissions me to spew unto the reader cataclysmal residuals of my mental precocity. The matter about which I am about to urp forth, complexicated a vast mass of field research, Internet analytics, laborious child interviews, consultations with sponsor marketers, and my own frequently untapped thought machine.

Early speakers of the English language colonized America in the late 15th century. [This was quite controversial in the youths' native England when their parents learnt of it. Colonization was widely unperformed in Europe and at the time was a regimental induction isolated to recently birthed Jewish boys alone.] Their composition studies took place in quaint schoolhouses and makeshift tree houses. According to termite-unscathed, sap-preserved writings on the walls, arboreal chirographic experts surmise that children learned composition by means of tapping their pencils into their papers like pointillism or medieval drills.

This tapping method evolved and mutated into strokes and lines, into block letters and cursive. The direness to modify ones elementary exercises to divert time lapses and modernity breaches is imperative to the transcendental regeneration of our offspring. Expedient evolution entails training and agreement to relinquish skeptics who disagree with us. Thus, civilized mankind must recognize that the time of the trained has arrived at the station.

In art and culture, schoolhouses have long been associated with warmth, with fuzzy feelings of goodness, with Popsicle stick crafts and storybook hours. The hardened cold truth is that the last Popsicle craft was built in 1983 by Miss Mayberry's 1st grade class at Stony Lane Elementary School in North Kingstown, Rhode Island, and the last storybook hour assembled in 1957 in Miss Gertrude's 4th grade class at The Good Shepherd School in Golden Valley, Minnesota.

Regretability—parental or unparental, pedagogue or apedagogue—may be arguable, but even the commonest of folk acquiesce that today's schoolhouse is a very different setting than it was in our day or back in 1492 when administrates mandated schoolgirls wear bonnets and schoolboys wear britches on premises.

Today, schoolhouse halls are rampant with terrors: Kindergartners wearing wash-on tattoos of violent arachnid and chiroptera superheroes; Second Graders lacing paper airplanes with postage stamps as passenger windows; Fifth Graders thinking juice cocktail is 100% juice; 7th Graders at lunch snorting boiled spaghetti noodles up their nostrils; and 8th Graders hole-punching their ear lobes and sticking titanium studs through the punctured flesh.

As educators, it is time to collect ourselves, reassemble and evolve. An overwhelming influx of A's supports that online college programs are the most efficacious vehicles for college students' academic enrichment and their parents'. We have tested the waters: It is time to integrate online education for grades K–8.

Hereith beneath I plant the curricular seed for the nearith forthcoming of juvenescence education as I foresee it:

THE PROGRAM

School Schedules

The children's daily schedules need not differ dramatically from a "normal" school day. Children will rise to their wake up call; march to breakfast and plop before the television set; perfunctorily dress (in school uniforms if an ecclesiastical institute); groom themselves with comb, brush, and toothpaste; bundle up if it's brisk; step out the front door; close the door; count to ten; open the door; enter back into the house; and fire up the computer.

Class will commence strictly at 9:00 am with the young students logging on with their unique User Identification (ID) and Password (PSWD) identifying themselves as present. (Students who log on late will be added to a tardy list. Students who sign on tardy more than three times a school year are subjected to stringent parental controls.)

A Glimpse at Curricula

Young grade school children will finger-paint on touch screen monitors; make collages of stock art in design programs; learn how to type lowercase letters by releasing the CAPS LOCK; and insert shapes like block arrows and flowcharts from word processing programs to evince geometrical grasp. (Hand-washing after using the bathroom will be based on the honor system. If suspicion of deceit is overt, keyboard swab tests will be executed.)

Older grade school children will practice their cursive by sweeping or swiping their computer mouse without lifting a finger; multiply and divide by learning how to copy and paste formulas into spreadsheets that generate the solutions; "Like" social media social studies; and author book reports upon perusing tabletified Electronic-books to minimize risk of paper cuts.

Middle school children will take timed placement tests that—by means of asterisks (SHIFT 8)—emulate the format of filling in dots with #2 lead pencil (an eraser will symbolically manifest itself in the form of a DEL key); dissect virtual harlequin frogs from The Sims: *Endangered Animals* PC game; learn Spanish and sex ed simultaneously by watching You Tubular media files of *Diego Animal Rescuer Wears Deodorant and Starts Shaving*; and ingest English Lit by listening to audio books of *Great Expectations* and *A Brave New World*.

A Highschool Reflection:
At this point in continuance, I do not advocate the integration of *high school* curricula into a purely online format. By eliminating the face-to-face interplay between high school students, the young adults lose the confines in which to meet like-minded, able-bodied peers and lose their virginity—a critical maneuver in the everlasting existence of mankind.

Granted, pundits of Medicine & Technology predict scientists will invent an electronic means for virginity forfeiture by path of simulation before college—and even possibly at the same time. (Soon enough we'll be growing babies in our gardens, and sexual intercourse will be a mere historical notion. Stories Grampa will tell your kids.)

Keeping in the Fun

Skeptics may scoff that school needs peppy, interactive activities to keep children's minds fresh, alert and percolating new brain cells. However, online elementary and middle school classes will integrate *fun* into *formula*. Just as in a normal school day, kids will enjoy Physical Education (P.E.). Modern technology has enabled computer users to interact—in real time—across a multitude of virtual sports platforms—from soccer to table tennis to fencing. With online P.E. there's no such thing as seasonal sports. Kids can play beach volleyball in the winter! (Middle school females enduring menstruation may eschew that week's activities by e-mailing the instructor a "." with scanned forensic sample.)

Choir, band, and drama are actionable with online schooling. Children rehearse via webcasts, and come recital time, parents are invited to their own home to login and listen to their child perform in synch with the other munchkinesqually groomed voices. Plays will be video-recorded for parents who come home late.

Extracurricular activities will be proffered such as fantasy football club; Google search races; classical keyboard lessons; Smartphone photography; field trips to online libraries; and Yearbook Club for blue screen class pictures.

Demographic Considerations and Controversies

Social interactional ostracization and hectoring will be an affliction of the past. With online classes, there will be no wedgies; no double dog dares or pulling hair; and no playground bullies. It is infeasible bullying be conducted via data processing machines; online bullying is a concept so impracticable that I employed zero research on the matter. Pushing a classmate's face off your screen will do nothing but break your computer; and kids needn't *wear* underwear when in attendance.

What about different demographic conditions (i.e., home lifestyle and ecopsycholoracential influencers)? Some children will have access to a grand patio sunroom with ergonomically crafted ottomans and wrist pads. While other children will be stationed in a windowless corners sitting stone cold on hard wooden benches or rocks. The privileged minorities' rooms will consistently sustain a comfy 72°F while other minorities' rooms will vacillate between a chilly 66 or a balmy 88. Propitiously, technology is ever-evolving: It be a "know brainer" that visionary inventors will engineer temperature-modifiable laptop speakers, wall breaker Windows, and comfy heated mouse pads large enough for the less fortunate children to snuggle into.

Composition theorist James Irving Berlin, states forth in his essay, "Rhetoric and Climatology in the Writing Class" that pupils cannot compositionally articulate their ideological values freely in stodgy, sterile classroom environments. I accede with this mindset. However, Berlin contends students need a wet environment to feel fresh to work well and expound. Now, that could be an electrical hazard for an online class—In particular, the cases where wireless access abstinence and unaffordability be employed. Therefore, I incline the reader to repel Berlin's fanciful notions about the wet part.

Theorist Good Lad Tobin approaches demographic inequalities from a famine-for-knowledge stance. In his essay "Eating Students, Eating Ourselves: Digesting the Teacher's Role in the Writing Class," he writes "Rhetorical sophistication is attainable by means of consuming students' minds without the theatrics of self-obsession." Tobin preaches that a teacher should be in close proximity to his student to consume ideas without bias. This is a laughable notion. Children are equally rechargeable batteries, and by 2028 teachers are all going to be robots anyway.

Can We Trust Them?

Opponents of online learning for K-8 cite the lack of parental whereabouts when the child is "attending" school *à la maison*. Working parents will not be at home to supervise the child, and stay-at-home parents—contrary to the moniker—have secret lives and don't really stay at home. Opponents voice fatiguing concerns for the children, indicating poor nutrition ("Children will eat cookies for lunch," they say); safety ("Children will find the hidden stash of detergent bullets and figure out how to load the dishwasher and chute"); and lack of discipline and Vitamin D.

Some opposing parents argue that their child will hibernate their computer as soon as the parents leave the house, and subject themselves to brain deadening, addictive soap operas marathons. Others argue their kid will get hooked on online video game playing—subsequently unable to shut down in the rare-but-precious moments when the family is home together for a sit-down dinner.

These absurd terrors are ludicrous and unfounded; the opposition's arguments are sheer non-profit anti-disbandment propaganda and a hush hush conspiracy steered by the Parent-Teacher Association (PTA). The PTA, dating back to its founding in 1897, has undeviatingly interfered in the schooling and scholarship of hundreds of millions of afore-potentialed children by corrupting their blank slates with huggy nurturing and community fostering as opposed to where the focus should be, which is on the wisdom imparted solidaritously by degreed Instructor.

I once referred to theorist Peter Ankle as an "Aristotle in modern dress." Yet, such a label better applies to yours truly. I, an educator, applaud online learning, and you parents, most likely are not teachers. "Those who educate children well are more to be honored than they who produce them; for these only gave them life, those the art of living well." In other words, I, Richard Fukerson, too wear woman's clothing.

Where Do We Go from Here?

This is another advantage of online schooling. We don't go anywhere.

Read Fukerson's full report "Make No Room for Kids: Bells Ding for Online Classes K-8" at Yale University's Beinecke Rare Book and Manuscript Library in New Haven, CT. The report is available in hard back only.

This work was sponsored by the University of Phonics, an innovative institution about to launch an exciting program for grades K-8, which, in the words of renowned composition theorist John Fukerson, Emeritus Texas A & M University, "An overwhelming influx of A's supports that online...programs are the most efficacious vehicles for...students' academic enrichment and their parents'."

If you would like to enroll your child in a trial run of a school year online, fill out the application downloadable at howtogofarwithoutgoinganywhereatall.com and mail it to 3157 E. Elwood St. 85034 with a signed mental liability release form.

Grade A Papers "Cheep Sheet"

This book is laced with whimsicalities:
random plays on words
random people—real and unreal
random events—actual and fictional
random references to movies, books, theater, art
and random randomnesses.

The "Cheep Sheet" sheds light on each paper's playful remarks and references.

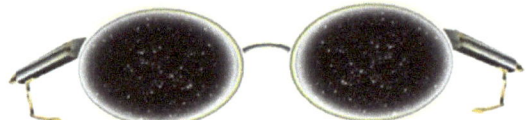

Grade A Papers "Cheep Sheet"
READING THE FINE GLINT

RED PEN ALERT: This document is CLASSIFIED. A Choose Your Own Misadventure.
- Annis Theesia sounds like "anesthesia."
- Armored skirts are a kind of tank armor.
- "....wann auch immer ich will" means "whatever I want" in German.
- In the movie "Amityville Horror" the possessed dad awakens at 3:15 each a.m.–the same time the man who *previously lived* in the house had taken an ax and committed a grisly murder.
- An ox is castrated and a bull is not.
- My dad drank *Schaefer* beer in the 70s and 80s.
- My dad was not exactly a master at remembering names.

- Thank you to **Sonya Jones** for designing the covers and laying out this book. I am so lucky to have worked with you on this project—from start to finish. This six month project turned into a year; you are my "partner in time" and a true talent!

Brokeback Mountain
- *Brokeback Mountain* was published in 1997 (not 1963). The story takes place in 1963.
- Heath Ledger won an Oscar for his role in "The Dark Knight" (not "Brokeback Mountain").
- Anne Hathaway was in "The Princess Diaries" (not "The Princess Bride").
- Annie Proulx (not Anne Proulix) is the writer. Ang Lee (not Lee Ang) is the director.

When I've Got No Class, I Stalk Famous Celebrities
- "Barbie Kendall" sounds like "Barbie Ken Doll".
- Justin Timberlake was in "The Mickey Mouse Club" (not "Bozo's Circus").
- Tom Hanks married Rita Wilson. Maria Shriver married Arnold Schwarzenegger. Hanks and Shriver do not have a child.
- "...didn't arrest my development!"– Jason Bateman was in "Arrested Development" TV series. Bateman's real life sister is Justine. She never got as famous as her brother.
- "The Breakfast Club" was filmed in Glenbrook High in Northbrook, IL. Estevez hooks up with Ally Sheedy.
- "Ellen's Dusty Diner" and "The Spotted Beacon" sound like the trendy Broadway restaurants "Ellen's Stardust Diner" and "The Spotted Pig."

Kaffka's *The Fly*, and Cronnenberg's "The Metamorphistufs" are totally GROSS.
- Oliver Sacks (not Slacks) wrote the book *The Man Who Mistook His Wife for a Hat* (not Gnat).
- Carole King wrote the musical "Really Rosie" (not "Free To Be You and Me"- not "Flea"). Carol Kane is an actress.
- Franz Kafka wrote *The Metamorphosis*. It's a story about a man who turns into a roach (not a fly). The book is in German (not Russian) and is titled *Die Verwandlung*. Franz was male.
- David Cronnenberg's movie "The Fly" is about a man who mutates into a human fly.
- "The Fly" and *The Metamorphosis* have no relation to each other.
- Gregor's sister plays the violin (not the cello).
- Gregor's dad throws apples at him (not pears).

Greek Mythology: Surreptitious and Submerged in the Celebrated Series Seinfeld
- All episodes and their scenes cited are real. The traits and personalities of the Greek characters are also real.

The Case of the Missing Pupils
- Piggy is a character in the book "Lord of the Flies." A boy breaks Piggy's glasses, and Piggy is later killed by a pack of boys with a boulder.

Burrr...There's a ~~Breeze~~ Draft in Here
- Miss Cellaneous sounds like "miscellaneous."
- Mr. Erieous *sounds like* "mysterious."
- "American Gothic" is a painting of a pitchfork-holding farmer beside his daughter (not wife).
- I burned this paper on my stovetop,

The History of American Horror Movies: From Tod Browning's GEEKS to M. Night Shamalamaham's THE SICK SCENT
- Thank you to **Udaykumar Gohel** for designing this graphic.
- Tod Browning directed "Freaks" (not "Geeks"). "Freaks" stars real life circus deformed performers (not nerds).
- M. Night Shyamalan (not Shamalamaham) directed "The Sixth Sense" (not "The Sick Scent").
- "I get chills, but they satisfy me" sounds like lyrics from "You're the One That I Want" – a song in the musical "Grease."
- Real titles are "Videodrome," "Clockwork Orange," "The Texas Chainsaw Massacre," "An American Werewolf in London," and "Halloween" (8 in the series).
- Orson Welles (not Arson) directed "Citizen Kane" (not "Citizen Pain"). In it an old man's last word is "Rosebud" (not "Noseblood") – his childhood sled.
- "...released a touch of evil on the set" - Orson Welles directed and acted in the movie "A Touch of Evil."
- The movie "Heathers" (not "Feathers") stars Winona Ryder and Christian Slater. In it, they coerce a popular, feathered-hair girl to drink drain cleaner.
- In the movie "Carrie," a girl dumps a bucket of pig's blood (not REDRUM) on Carrie. REDRUM and blood pouring out of elevators is from "The Shining."
- In "Psycho," Janet Leigh's (not Kathy Bates') character showers at The Bates Motel. Kathy Bates takes a nude dip in a hot tub in "About Schmidt."
- "The Blair Witch Project" was filmed in an American woods.
- Joanne Woodward acted as a woman with three personalities (not faces) in "Three Faces of Eve."
- In "Seven," a decapitated head (of Brad Pitt's character's girlfriend) is packed in a box (not a hatbox)."Starved Wars" sounds like "Star Wars."
- Alfred (not Adolf) Hitchcock directed "The Birds," but not "To Kill a Mockingbird." The movies are unrelated.
- In "To Kill a Mockingbird," Gregory Peck plays Atticus Finch (not Flinch). "...shouting 'Boo!'"– Boo Radley is another character in the film.
- "Sweeney Todd" is a musical about a murderous barber and his lady-friend Mrs. Lovett. They kill and cook people and serve them to unknowing customers. The story is not about zombies. "They're coming to get you, Barbara" (not Barber) is from the zombie movie "Night of the Living Dead." "Nothing's Going to Harm You" (not "Eat You") is from a song in "Sweeney Todd." "Ba da da da da, I'm lovin' it" is a popular McDonalds jingle.
- "Blairingly evident" (not glaringly) sounds like Linda Blair. Blair plays the possessed child Regan in "The Exorcist." Regan's head spins around in a full circle. Regan sounds like Republican President Reagan.

The History of American Horror Movies: From Tod Browning's GEEKS to M. Night Shamalamaham's THE SICK SCENT (continued)

- "Dead Ringers" (not "Dead Slingers") stars Jeremy Irons. He plays sadistic twin gynecologists. Theresa Russell was not in "Dead Ringers," but was in "Black Widow," in which she played a serial husband-killer.
- "He who walks behind the rows" is the real slogan for "Children of the Corn."
- Mia Farrow plays the mother of the devil's baby in "Rosemary's Baby." Farrow and Woody Allen were a real life couple who parted when Allen hooked up with Farrow's adopted daughter.
- Heidi Sorenson, 1981 Playmate of the Month, had one scene (topless) in "Fright Night."
- David Morse (not Remorse) is the actor in "Disturbia." Morse's character wears a wig in one scene to make it appear the woman he murdered is still alive. Michael Caine played a killer in drag in "Dressed to Kill."
- In "Nightmare on Elm Street" (not "Pet Dreams on Elm Street") the evil character is Freddy Krueger (not Cujor). Cujo was a killer dog (not sheepdog). In "Nightmare on Elm Street" the slogan is "Whatever you do, don't fall asleep" (not "Whatever you do, don't maul a sheep").
- "Gigli" is a romantic comedy that bombed at the box office. It has a notorious reputation of being one of the worst romantic comedies ever made. It won six Razzie awards. The Razzies is a real awards ceremony that recognizes the worst movies of the year.
- Clark Gable (not Darth Gable- which sounds like Darth Vader) was in "It Happened One Night" (not "Fright"). It won five Academy Awards in 1935.
- "A genius movie maker with many blockbusters ahead of him" is a joke because Shyamalan thus far (2013) has made a series of flops following "The Sixth Sense."
- The big surprise at the end of "The Sixth Sense" is that the character played by Bruce Willis is actually a ghost. Throughout the movie the audience thinks he's alive. (There is nothing about decomposition in the movie.)
- The scratch marks on the last page were spread with red finger paint on a paring knife.

Is this Advanced Primate Psychology? I think I may be in the wrong class...

- Thank you **Mrvic Goran** for designing this graphic of Goodall and Rand...and the chimp.
- Chianti is an Italian wine. "Bouteille" is French for "bottle."
- Gestalt psychology is observing things in their entirety before focusing on individual elements.
- Avoidance learning is an actionable response to avoid an undesired result.
- Operant conditioning is awarding someone for a desired action to achieve results.
- Reverse psychology involves advocating an opposite position in order to achieve the desired result.
- Gibbons have almost hairless faces. Male gibbons have white patches on their faces. Female gibbons have black patches on their heads.
- Freud's ID is the part of the mind that contains a human's instinctual drives like sex and aggression.
- Gibbons have ball and socket joints which provide flexibility in swinging. Gibbons are arboreal. Gibbons eat primarily fruit. Gibbons are monogamous.
- Countries where gibbons live include China and northeast India.
- Freud's Oedipus complex is a desire for sexual involvement with the parent of the opposite sex.
- Free association is when one word or image may suggest another without a direct connection. Psychoanalysis is exploration into the subconscious.
- Cognitive dissonance theory suggests that we have an inner drive that desires harmony in beliefs and and opinions.
- Belief disconfirmation occurs when a person is presented with information that conflicts with their beliefs.
- Social behaviorism is behavior directed towards society or members of the same species.
- Chimps knuckle walk on all fours. The common chimp gets antagonistic. However, bonobos work out their squabbles by means of copulation.
- Jane Goodall is a primatologist known for her 45 year study of social interactions of wild chimps. The statement listed is a genuine quote of Goodall's.
- Ayn Rand was a philosopher who supported rational and ethical egoism. The statement listed is a genuine quote of Rand's.

Invasion of the Faculty Snatchers

- "Invasion of the Body Snatchers" is a famous horror movie about aliens that grow in pods that invade earth-starting with San Francisco.

Tenureless Voices: An Awe Filled Lot of Adjuncts in America

- Adjuncts are part time, untenured teachers. "An Awe Filled Lot" sounds like "an awful lot."
- Professor Udon, Flamenco University (and any such study) are fully fictional. My dad drew the two cartoons (self portraits).
- 3+6+8+1+4+2+1+3= 28, not 27
- The state abbreviation for Missouri is MO not MS. University of Buffalo is in New York, but not New York City.
- "Oguh" is Hugo spelled backwards. Melba and Rye ("Wry") are types of bread. Paige Turner sounds like "page turner."
- Annie "Peacepenny" is a name play on Little Orphan Annie who is adopted by Daddy "Warbucks." "The Moon Goes Down on Yesterdays" sounds like a song from the musical Annie: "The Sun Will Come Out Tomorrow."
- The Pulitzer Prize is the prestigious award for writers. Publishers Clearinghouse runs a prize-driven game to sell merchandise.
- Wong Invet Mint sounds like "wrong investment." Doonesbury comics are politically left-leaning.
- Fay Lee Unst-Haybell sounds like "fairly unstable."
- "Pick Udon's noodle" is a word play because, while noodle stands for "brain," Udon is a kind of thick noodle.

King Kong Steals Professor's Pay Day and Ascends Vending Machine

- In the movie "King Kong," Fay Wray is the actress who plays the desired woman that King Kong snatches. He climbs to the top of the Empire State Building with the woman in his clutches. Fay Wray" rhymes with "Pay Day." Pay Day is a kind of candy bar.

Stuffed between Heaven and Hell: Is Taco Bell Are Savior or the Devil Incarnitas?

- "Stuffed" between sounds like "stuck between." "Devil Incarnitas" sounds like "Devil Incarnate."
- Jewel, Dominic and Aldie are—or resemble—names of grocery stores. Cardot sounds like "card." Jewel (the grocery store) used to have "Jewel Cards" for product discounts.
- "Towel or Rinse" sounds like "Tolerance."

I Will Not Let My Willow Weep

- Thank you to **Udaykumar Gohel** for designing this graphic.

My pHd is fur the Sabbathical, not the Celery

- Thank you to **Udaykumar Gohel** for designing this graphic.
- Hilly thinks a sabbatical is a "sabbathical." When Hilly writes "celery," she means "salary." She thinks Ph.D.'s who take sabbaticals are missionaries.
- Hilly Rae-Lime sounds like "(The) Hills Are Alive"—a song from "The Sound of Music." During this song Julie Andrews plays a singing nun dancing in the hills.
- Northwestern (Evanston, Illinois) is one of the top universities in the U.S.
- CLC has a branch in Vernon Hills (not Vermin Hills).
- "I want mine will go to II" sounds like a line from "Spinal Tap."
- Lourdes is in France, not Switzerland. It is a place of pilgrimage. Ill people travel to Lourdes in hopes that—by anointing themselves with the holy Lourdes water—that they will be healed.
- In Europe, women bathing topless (not "bottomless") is accepted on public beaches.
- Julie Andrews played a nanny (not a nun) in "Mary Poppins."
- Picasso, Van Gogh, Monet, and Toulouse Lautrec were artists who painted in the Montmartre district in Paris, France (not Rio, Brazil).
- My dad drew the quirky cartoon of himself as Toulouse Lautrec, which I inserted into the bubble-making him the shepherd.
- Sangria is a Spanish fruity alcoholic beverage (not a country).
- Prostitution is legal in Holland.
- "Free at Last" is from Martin Luther King's "I Have a Dream" speech.

Java Script: An alarming report on the direty for coasters in computer labs

- Morris Cold sounds like "Morse Code."
- Underwriters Laboratories is a product/safety testing lab in Northbrook, Illinois.
- Caribou is a coffeehouse chain known for its comfy armchairs.
- Area 51 is a mysterious air force base.
- I used a mug and a fake rubber rat to make a ring and prints with instant coffee. Thanks for your help, Tony!

On Auragin of Theses

- Charles Darwin wrote *On Origin of Species* about natural selection.
- Fauna is the animal. Flora is the plant.
- Thank you to **Tóth Attila** for designing these graphics.
- Sam Serriff sounds like the font type "San Serif." This paper is typed in MS San Serif.
- Delta Community College is in Moorhead, Mississippi. Johnny Russell is from Moorhead.
- Wanda A. Roundalott sounds like "wander around a lot."
- "10 cents an advance" sounds like the Rodgers & Hart song "Ten Cents a Dance."
- Indian Hills Community College was called Iowa Tech. Part of it is called Airport Campus.
- Porta Poitier sounds like "porta potty."
- Mid-Plains College is the oldest college in Nebraska.
- E.T. Elliott sounds like the movie "E.T." The alien E.T. befriends a boy named Elliot.

This paper contains the Origins of the Universe —Literately

- Thank you to **Donna Harriman Murillo** for designing these graphics.
- An "Epiphany" is when you suddenly realize something amazing and life changing. "Dunno" sounds like "don't know." The character Epiphany Dunno is a clueless character with a touch of oblivious brilliance.
- Bernstein and Woodward were co-reporters on the Watergate scandal.
- *The Courier Gazette* and the *Camden Herald* are real newspapers.
- Leon means "Lion" in Greek.
- Isaac Newton theorized about laws of motion and gravitational force. Newton said that watching an apple fall from a tree was the first thing that got him wondering about gravity. The myth is that the apple fell on his head and triggered his scientific epiphany.
- The prince from Greece is Leon King of Sparta.
- Pi (in Greek) is the ratio: 3.141592+, measuring the circumference of a circle to its diameter.
- *A Wrinkle in Time* is a science fiction fantasy novel.
- The sample of the universe at the end of this paper is a Fig Newton smear.

Hall Bell Has Broken Loose! Has Anybody Seen Alfredo? Or: The Alarming Tale of a Missing Exchange Student...

- My dad also taught adjunct at Barat College in Lake Forest, Illinois.
- "All Bell Has Broken Loose!" sounds like "All Hell Has Broken Loose!"
- It may be inferred that Sammy Black is Cherry Black's little brother.
- It makes no sense that Velma says she's missing her half locket—because she just took it out.
- Names Velma and Wilma sound similar and are easy to confuse. Both are cartoon character names (Velma from "Scooby Doo," and Wilma from "The Flintstones").
- Gwen and Jill are characters in a kids' book series "Something Queer is Going On..." (1973-1997). They are young sleuths.
- The character Dean Dean Dean is in the good spirit of the book *Catch 22's*: 'Major Major' and the movie "Airplane's": 'Roger Roger.'
- This is the love square: Velma cheated on Alfredo with Peter. Peter cheated on Harmonia with Velma. At the end, Velma wrongly thinks that Alfredo and Peter were lovers.
- Janitor Jack knew that Professor Potbelly ate Alfredo (all except his arm) and agrees to keep it under wraps for a promotion to night watchman. Potbelly gets away with the crime and is elected to the School Board.

Astroprojection in the Classroom: A Credit-Wurthy Feet

- Thank you to **Udaykumar Gohel** for designing this graphic.
- Mary Maladies sounds like the "Merrie Melodies" cartoons.
- "Creative Friction" sounds like "Creative Fiction."
- The first lines are reminiscent of Georgia O'Keefe and her cloud paintings. Aviator Amelia (not Bedelia) Earhart (not Airhart) disappeared into the clouds.

The Intrinsic Quandary of Unionizing Interns

Teacher, please introdouche me 2 hot girl in the 1st row???.....

"Time Outs" Made Me A Better Man

- Donnie Muhwee sounds like "Donny Marie" like the Osmonds brother and sister duo.
- Lancers is the name of CLC's deli.
- Medusa's hair is snakes.
- Gurnee Mills is a shopping mall in Gurnee, Illinois.

The Little Engine That Couldn't

- It's true my dad did not realize this was a fake paper. He marked it up (without giving it a grade) at the train depot cafe pictured in the photo.
- Twice I reference the waitress saying "Enjoy" to the bearded man. This was a joke between my dad and our family. We all thought it sounded awkward when servers tell you to "enjoy" your food, so we turned it into a joke.
- Pedal and Cup is on the outskirts of Lake Geneva, Wisconsin. Lake Geneva is a resort town. The killer in the paper escapes from the "lake resort town."
- "Deepest river in the state" is similar to "deepest lake in the state." Geneva Lake is said to be Wisconsin's deepest lake - not counting Lake Michigan or Superior.

I treat Bell so Well; So why is my Fairy so Mythed?

- "Mythed" sounds like "miffed"—as in angry.
- Cupcake Doll, Blossom Doll, Glitter Hair Barbie, and Toddler Barbie Swingset are real toys.
- My son colored in the drawings.

- Jeremiah Toed sounds like the "Jeremiah was a Bullfrog" song.
- "Cloudy and Chair" sounds like "Sonny and Cher."
- Anita's hair is courtesy of a Barbie, a black Sharpie marker and glue.

Pinocchio Malwired: The Leftover Secret Code

- Thank you to **Fabio Fantini** for creating this egg graphic.
- The secret code is that each letter is offset one key to the right on a QWERTY keyboard. For example, "a" is "s" because "s" is one key to the right of "a". (You have to move the letter over to the left to decode the student's paper.
- This is QWERTY's paper decoded:

> "I am a robot, not a student. I always wanted to be a real boy. I come to school to learn how. I broke down last week in the lunch line. I bring my food to school now. I'm not the type to waste. Now I type leftovers. Invite me over. If someone would only figure me out, I'd be right

- Thank you to **Fabio Fantini** for designing this glasses/pen/universe egg-eyes graphic.

From Stall Secureity to the Hippo Campus: How to Make Collage a Better Insditution

- Thank you to **Julizar Hakim** for designing these 10 images.
- *Always Friends Club: Cricket Goes to the Dogs* is a young adult book by Susan Meyers about a dog wash.
- *A Prayer for Owen Meany* is a novel by John Irving.
- "Tinned curry" sounds like the actor "Tim Curry."
- Charles Darwin (not Charmin, which is a brand of toilet paper) thought up the "Survival of the Fittest" (not "Dimmest") theory.
- The CLC map resembles the actual campus layout.
- The last three lines of the paper sound like lyrics from the "What a Wonderful World" song.

My mom wrote this paper. I'm so embarrassed.

- Donna's lipstick kiss is courtesy of mi hermana.

Please Professor, hold me back after class! The Mob in the Hall is Closing in on Me!!!

- Thank you **Mrvic Goran** for creating these designs.
- Ana Mona Pia sounds like "onomatopoeia."
- Kiddieland (1929-2009) was an amusement park in a West Chicago suburb.
- Professor Higgins is a character from "My Fair Lady." He teaches a cockney woman to speak eloquently.
- "Creative Diction" sounds like "Creative Fiction."
- Gandalf is a character from the book *Lord of the Rings*. Middle Earth is a place in *Lord of the Rings*. Gandhi was a peaceful Hindu from India and was a vegetarian.
- Ewansiha and Obike are Nigerian names for boys. Ewansiha means "secrets cannot be bought" and Obike means "strong household."
- Windhoek is in Namibia, Africa. Narnia is a fictional setting for C.S. Lewis's *The Chronicles of Narnia*.

- Thank you to **Julizar Hakim** for designing these 8 graphics.

booksonawhim.com

The Nutty Years of the Jon Stewart Presidency in a Nutshell

Part I

OBAMA RESIGNS TO HAWAII

Obama Brushes Off Birth Certificate

- "The Amazing Race" is a reality TV show where contestants travel around the world looking for clues that lead them to other destinations—and ultimately $1,000,000.
- "The Apprentice" is a reality TV show led by conservative billionaire Donald Trump. Trump has challenged the authenticity of Obama's birth certificate.

The First Lady Thrusts

- Michelle Obama is known for launching fitness campaigns—especially geared toward youth.
- The Jane Fonda video and thrust movement referred to are real.

A RESURRECTED ELECTION

- In the 1990 TV show "Twin Peaks," the main character Laura Palmer speaks in an unintelligible, supernatural tongue. The last episode leaves the viewers hanging (like an apple on a tree): Agent Cooper is possessed by the evil spirit Bob.
- Joe Biden was accused of plagiarizing a speech during his presidential run in 1988.

Republican Primary

- *The Magic Mountain* is a novel by Thomas Mann that takes place at a sanatorium in Switzerland.
- According to many, the year of Creation was 4414 B.C. Perry supports teaching Creationism in schools.
- A study in May of 2012 announced results to support a theory that dinosaur flatulence emitted methane into the air and led to the species' extinction. The headline referred to was the real headline in *Current Biology*.
- Clint Eastwood did a (widely panned) skit at the 2012 Republican National Convention during which he talked to an empty chair—pretending Obama was sitting on it.

Democratic Primary

- Hillary Clinton's 2008 campaign TV ad was real. The line "It's 3 a.m...." is from the ad.
- Edward Snowden was a National Security Agency contractor who revealed that the NSA and Verizon were capturing Americans' cell phone data.
- "Play a nice game of Solitaire" is a line from "The Manchurian Candidate." Whenever the lead character hears this line, he becomes brainwashed, and his brainwashing leads him to commit murder.
- "Have you checked the children?" is a line from "When a Stranger Calls." In the movie the babysitter receives creepy phone calls from a killer—who it turns out is in the house with her.
- Philanthropist Chelsea Clinton married a wealthy investment banker and bought an apartment in Manhattan for $10.5 MM. "Moving On Up" is the theme song from the TV show "The Jeffersons."

Democratic Primary- continued

- The actors listed as George Clooney supporters are really Democrats. The list is a spoof on the "Six Degrees of Kevin Bacon" game.
- Cary Grant was a secret homosexual who tried to cover it up by marrying and pretending to be straight. It was generally known in Hollywood that he was gay, and his peers helped keep it a secret to protect his career. There have been rumors that Clooney is pulling the same stunt.
- Before he was famous, Clooney had a role on "The Facts of Life" TV show as a handyman. Mrs. Garrett is a housemother in the show.
- Former Illinois governor Rob Blagojevich was wiretapped and recorded as saying "I've got this thing and it's f***ing golden"—referring to his power to fill the Senate vacancy seat left by Obama. Willy Wonka is a storybook character that hides golden tickets into chocolate bars.

The Zeppo Marx Roast

- Zeppo Marx actually died in 1979. But had he lived he would have been 98 in 1999—the year Jon Stewart's "The Daily Show" launched.
- Marx is notoriously known as being the only Marx Brother of the four that was not at all funny. His brothers Groucho, Chico and Harpo were hilarious.
- In 2002, documentarian Michael Moore harshly interviewed then elderly actor Charlton Heston. Charleston Chew is a candy bar.

ART AND MONEY: CHAMPAGNE FINANCE

Chicago Billionaires OutsmART Chicago Mayor

- I mailed this version of *Grade A Papers* (as Volume 2) to The Griffins—a real billionaire couple in Chicago.
- Actor Vince Vaughn is a Republican from Chicago.
- The Chicago Art Institute houses Henri Matisse's "Bathers by a River" and Man Ray's "Chess Set." ("One Night in Bangkok" is a song from the musical "Chess.") Jackson Pollack was an abstract painter who has several of works displayed at the Chicago Art Institute. His paintings are intricate, incomprehensible and consist of chaotic lines, colorful swirls and frenetic strokes.
- The Griffins did donate $19 MM to the construction of the Art Institute's new modern wing in 2006.
- Mayor Rahm Emanuel spearheaded the effort to close 49 Chicago public schools in 2013.

Chicago Mayor OutsmARTS Chicago Billionaires

- I mailed this version of *Grade A Papers* (as Volume 3) to Mayor Rahm Emanuel.
- Ken Griffin is president of Citadel, a hedge fund company. CITGO is a gas station.
- Charles Lafitte Rosé is a cheap champagne. Beaujolais—despite being celebrated in France as the year's first harvest—is (arguably) a poor wine.
- Anne Griffin is French. "872 North State Street just off the Red Line" is the address of "Frenchy's Adult Bookstore."

Thank you to **Donna Harriman Murillo** for designing this Presidents Playhouse graphic.

Thank you to **Solidesign** for designing this White House column graphic.

Chicago Mayor OutsmARTS Chicago Billionaires- Continued

- Ken Griffin purchased the abstract painting "False Start" for $80 MM. It was painted by American contemporary artist Jasper Johns. "False Start" is an abstract mishmash of colors. The Abrakadoodle Art Studio for Kids is a real studio in Singapore where children take art classes.
- Actor Owen Wilson supported Hillary Clinton's presidential run in 2008. Wilson and Vaughn starred together in the movie "The Wedding Crashers."
- A famous Chicago statue is "Cloud Gate" in Millennium Park. However, it is widely known as "The Bean."
- The Smith Museum of Stained Glass is a real museum at Chicago's Navy Pier.

THE DEBATES

Mount Rushmore Face-Off

- In the mid-sixties, Mitt Romney attended Cranbrook Institute—a prep school for boys—in Michigan. When Romney was a student, he pinned down a boy who had long hair and cruelly cut it off.
- Obama gave a startlingly lackluster performance during his first debate against Romney in 2012. (Obama debated against John McCain in 2008.)
- In his book *Dreams of My Father*, Obama recalls "smoking pot in a van."

A Staged Debate

- Actress Kim Cattrall lent her voice to a Manhattan GPS system—using the sexy voice of her character Samantha in the TV show "Sex and the City."
- Kraine Theater is a tiny, off-off-Broadway experimental theater in Manhattan.
- Jar Jar Binks is an annoying character from "Star Wars: The Clone Wars."
- Paul Ryan obsessively sipped water during his vice presidential debate against Biden in 2012. "...search party on a quest to save Ryan located him in private" sounds like "Saving Private Ryan."

STEWART'S INAUGURATION AND EXECUTIVE OUTFIT

The Assassination Attempt and the Spaceballs Alien

- Annie Leibovitz is a famous photographer. She and Stewart never married.
- In a contentious 2004 interview on the CNN news show "Crossfire," Stewart enraged host Tucker Carlson by calling Carlson out on "Crossfire's" biased, sensationalistic reporting. Carlson was 35 at the time and wore a bow tie. "Crossfire" was taken off the air shortly after the Stewart interview.
- Singer Janet Jackson alleges she experienced a "wardrobe malfunction" that revealed her breast at the XXXVIII Super Bowl Halftime Show.
- In the movie "Alien," an alien bursts out of actor John Hurt's character's stomach. In Mel Brooks' parody "Spaceballs," Hurt makes a guest appearance in a diner scene. In this scene, an alien bursts out of Hurt's stomach. The alien dons a top hat and cane and sings "Ragtime Gal" on the counter.

Colbert's Silent Tongue

- In the TV series "Downton Abbey," a character slips on a bar of soap to tragic results.
- Donald O'Connor and Gene Kelly starred in "Singing in the Rain." In this movie, their characters devise a scheme where an actress lip-synchs to the voice of another woman. In a famous scene the other woman stands behind as curtain as the actress pretends to sing on stage.
- Bill O'Reilly is a conservative political commentator who has appeared on "The Colbert Report." Colbert's mock persona on "The Colbert Report" is modeled after O'Reilly.

Samantha's Bees and John's Olives

- Best Buy's (an appliance store) technical support team is called "The Geek Squad." Bed, Bath and Beyond is a retail store.
- Vladimir Putin passed a law in December 2012 that prohibits Americans from adopting children in Russia.
- You can only get to Kamchatka, Russia by sea or air.
- "Please Sir, I want some more" is a line from the book *Oliver Twist*—which is a tale about an English orphan named Oliver.
- Miss Hannigan is the mean proprietor of an orphanage in the musical "Annie." In one scene she pours gin into her bathtub.

Stewart's Cabinet Unhinged

- Conan O'Brien did a skit where he pretended to run across the country (from New York City to Los Angeles) to accept the job of "Late Night" host—replacing Jay Leno. Due to lackluster reviews, O'Brien only lasted seven months in the role.
- O'Brien, Stewart and Colbert once staged a mock feud: "Who Made Mike Huckabee."
- "Solo dad" sounds like "Soledad." Soledad O'Brien is a broadcast journalist unrelated to Conan.
- Cheatham County Community Theater is a real theater in Kingston Springs, Tennessee.
- Fresh Pond Mall is a real shopping center in Cambridge, Massachusetts.
- Dolly Parton played a secretary in "9 to 5" which takes place in New York City.
- "Dear Abby" is an advice column.
- Elle Décor is a home décor company.
- Miss Daisy is a character in the movie "Driving Miss Daisy," in which she is driven around by a chauffeur.
- Jack Sparrow is the name of the lead pirate character in "Pirates of the Caribbean."
- John McCain served in Vietnam. He had an affair during his first marriage.
- Demeter—in Greek Mythology—is Goddess of the Harvest. For six months each year, her beloved daughter is imprisoned in the Underworld. In grief, Demeter neglects the harvest during these six months each year—causing winter. She returns to the harvest when she has her daughter back.

GLOBAL FRICTION AND OTHER TALES OF DISASTER

The Amazon Plant Invasion

- The notion of man-eating plants comes from the show "Little Shop of Horrors." In this musical, Venus flytrap-like plants consume and conquer earth.
- There is a song in the musical called "Don't Feed the Plants."

An Infestation of Tics Down Under

- "The Wiggles" is a musical group that performs kids songs. They have a song called "Big Red Car." In their official music video, Jeff Fratt (one of "The Wiggles") falls asleep in the back seat.
- Tony Abbott is the Prime Minister of Australia. Elvis Costello (singer) sounds like Abbott and Costello (vaudeville duo).

McDonalds Serves Freedom Flies

- In 2003 U.S. officials renamed "French Fries" to "Freedom Fries" in three Congressional cafeterias in protest against France's opposition to the War in Iraq.
- "The Mold War" sounds like "The Cold War."
- In 2013, McDonalds salads only made up to 3 percent of all orders.
- Joan of Arch sounds like Joan of Arc, the French folk heroine.

The Incorporation of Congress and the Inferiority Complex of the SEC

- "Occupy Wall Street" was a protest movement. "Wall Street: Money Never Sleeps" was a sequel to the movie "Wall Street" starring Michael Douglas as Gordon Gekko.

Part II

ROMANTIC ESCAPADES AND THE NSA

The Sexting Scandal of Petraeus and Paula

- Former CIA Director David Petraeus had an affair with his biographer, Paula Broadwell (not Paula Abdul the singer).
- Petraeus and Broadwell would jog together in Afghanistan (not rollerblade).
- John Inglis (not Linglis) is Director of the NSA.

E-Dating Hackers Spread Virus

- President George W. Bush claimed there were weapons of mass destruction.
- The quotes about Mercury poisoning are real from online forums.
- Hermes is a messenger in Greek Mythology who delivers messages between the Gods and the Mortals. Hermes is known as Mercury in Roman Mythology.
- "It's Just Lunch" (not "It's Just Punch") is a real dating service that arranges for singles to meet face-to-face for lunch.

The Study Abroad Tax Evasion Scandal

- Hofbräuhaus, Brasserie Julien and Restaurante Figueira Rubaiyat are famous restaurants in Germany, France and Brazil.
- 餓孩 in 香 means "Starving Children" in "China."

The Clothing of Guantanamo

- Actress Sigourney Weaver battles in mechanical robot gear in "Aliens." Weaver also starred in "Ghost Busters." In "Ghost Busters" the Stay Puft Marshmallow Boy terrorizes New York City.

Italy Loses Color

- San Marino and the Vatican City are independent cities states—they are not considered a part of Italy despite their being landlocked by it. (Sicily and Sardinia are parts of Italy.)
- Frederico Fellini was an Italian director whose films include "8 1/2" and "La Dolce Vita"—two black and white art films in the 1960s.

The Controversial Erection of the BOLLYWOOD Sign in Tirumala

- Director Danny Boyle directed "Trainspotting" and "Slum Dog Millionaire."
- The child actors in "Slum Dog Millionaire" were poorly compensated despite the film's success.
- "Good Will Bunting" sounds like "Good Will Hunting"—a movie by director Gus Van Sant.
- "Boost" is a popular chocolate-flavored kids drink in India.

Part III — DOMESTICATED NUISANCES AND A CRAZY LITTLE THING CALLED WAR

Giving America the New Bird
- Brenda Starr is a comic book character—a glamorous, redheaded investigative reporter.
- The journal quotes about the African Grey Parrot are legit.

A Crockpot of Bull And the Texas Secession
- 25,000 signatures are needed in order for the Federal Government to respond to a petition. Texas's petition to secede from the U.S. exceeded the 25,000 mark in 2012.
- Thomas Edison owned the "Electric Light Company" (not the "Electric Write Company").
- San Antonio and Austin are democratically leaning cities in a staunchly Republican state.
- "Embrace puns and clay pigeons" sounds like "embrace guns and religion."
- Waxy O'Connor's is a real Irish Pub on the Riverwalk in San Antonio.
- "Austin City Limits" is a famous radio show.
- Davy Crockett (not Crocker) did not marry Betty Crocker. Betty Crocker is not even a real person, but an American icon for baking. "...married baker Betty" sounds like "Mary Baker Eddy"—the founder of Christian Science.

AN ECONOMIC COLLAPSE AND ITS NIPPLE EFFECT

The Rise and Fall of the White Bread Factory: Cutting Off The Trust
- The lead male character in the movie "Boogie Nights" is well-endowed.
- The biggest layoffs during the Recession included General Motors, City Group, Merrill Lynch and JP Morgan Chase.
- There were 9,177,877 whites living in Illinois according a 2012 census.

Part IV

THE PRESIDENTS PLAYHOUSE

The White House is a Fun House: From Remote Control Drones to "Being John Edwards"
- "Yes, We Can" was Obama's campaign slogan during his 2008 presidential run.
- During his presidency, Ronald Reagan launched the Strategic Defense Initiative, which was also known as Star Wars. It was an anti-ballistic missile defense program that was set up in 1984.
- David Axelrod was a presidential advisor to Obama. Axl Rose was the lead singer of "Guns n' Roses."

Fraggles Fuss About Fracking
- Stewart really did appear as a guest on "Sesame Street" and Miss Piggy really did drop by "The Daily Show."
- HBO and CBC were the two cable channels that carried "Fraggle Rock."

The Perfume Wars
- The Swiss are known for being neutral—not opinionated.

HEALTH AND EPIDEMICS

The Whore on Drugs
- The Palmer family's chef is really rumored to be the inventor of the brownie.
- Bertha Palmer's husband's first name is Potter.
- Auguste Rodin's famous sculpture is "The Kiss" (not "The Genital Kiss"). Rodin sculpted dogs, but not humping dogs.
- Rodin actually did sculpt Bertha Palmer, but not in the likeness of a headless bust.
- Sculptress Camille Claudel was Rodin's lover. She was very jealous—but her jealousy was over other women, not who sculpted them.
- "Fear and loafing for lost wages" sounds like *Fear and Loathing in Las Vegas*—a book about strung out road-trippers.

Obama-Éclair (The Affordable Heath Bar Act) and the Smithsonian Sweet Tooth
- On June 28, 2012 the Supreme Court held up the statute for the Affordable Care Act.
- "A movable sweet" sounds like "a movable feast."
- American business owners with more than 49 employees must provide health care benefits.
- Diana Ross was the lead singer of "The Supremes" girl group. Another girl group during the same era was "Candy and the Kisses."
- In 1981, Sandra Day O'Connor became the first woman appointed to the Supreme Court.
- Actress Sharon Stone plays a character in "Basic Instinct" who grabs the attention of her interrogators by uncrossing her legs to show she's not wearing underwear.

The White House is a Fun House: From Remote Control Drones to "Being John Edwards" - Continued
- In Oscar Wilde's novel *The Picture of Dorian Gray*, a portrait of the protagonist ages, but the protagonist does not. He watches himself get older in the painting, although in "real life" he does not age throughout the years.
- In the movie "Being John Malkovich," people crawl through a portal into actor Malkovich's brain. They co-exist in Malkovich's brain and body. John Edwards, former senator and vice presidential candidate, has a sordid past of infidelity and smarminess.

The Presidents Playhouse: A Cellar Discovery
- On June 11, 1962 Frank Morris (with two other prisoners) escaped from Alcatraz by chipping away at his jail cell wall with tools—creating a secret passage he crawled through.

The Mississippi Missile Crisis
- "An officer and a gentlewoman" sounds like the movie "An Officer and a Gentleman."
- Aruba rhymes with Cuba.

The Regeneration of the Smartphone into the Human Hand
- The first smartphone was really named Simon. It was invented by IBM in 1992. According to *USA Today*, "IBM borrows twice as much money as it earns annually."
- There is an old superstition that if you drop a fork, it means someone is coming to visit.
- Daniel Day Lewis is an acclaimed actor who possesses a unique ability to play dramatically different roles. He starred in the movie "My Left Foot."

The Long Term Effects of Lasik Come to Light
- May 13 is singer Stevie Wonder's birthday.
- Both Wonder and Ray Charles are blind. Charles is more highly respected as a serious musician than Wonder.
- The whites of the eyes is called "sclera," not "scareras."
- The highest note ever sung was by Maria Aloysia Antonia Weber in Mozart's "Popoli di Tessaglia" concerto in 1777.

The Presidents Playhouse: A Cellar Discovery - Continued
- There is a contemporary classical composer named John Adams. He composed an opera called "Nixon in China."
- Former White House intern Monica Lewinsky fooled around with a cigar under Bill Clinton's watchful guard.
- Spiro Agnew was disbarred.
- Millard Fillmore started the White House library.
- Harvey Milk was gay. Barbara Pierce Bush is gay.
- Franklin Delano Roosevelt used a wheelchair. Andrew Jackson used a hickory cane.
- Actress Marilyn Monroe sang seductively to John F. Kennedy on his 45th birthday.
- Richard Nixon lied like Pinocchio. Clinton plays the sax.
- In 1992 Dan Quayle misspelled potato on TV.
- Lincoln was assassinated at a theater.
- Warren G. Harding gambled away White House china in a poker game.

- Ronald Reagan loved jelly beans.
- "I would gladly pay you Tuesday for a hamburger today" is a line from the Popeye comic strip and movie. It's spoken by Wimpy—a portly (like Taft) scam artist.
- "Harlequin Head" is a painting by Picasso that was stolen.
- Andy Warhol featured unopened soup cans in his paintings.
- A chaise lounge is part of the action in director Stanley Kubrick's "Eyes Wide Shut" orgy scene.
- Grover Cleveland got married in the White House.
- Woodrow Wilson ratified the 19th amendment—allowing women the right to vote.
- Theodore Roosevelt—a conservative—was nonetheless an avid supporter of labor unions.
- Former French Prime Minister Francois Mitterand openly split his time between his wife and his mistress.
- Michael Dukakis ran unsuccessfully for president in 1988.
- Actor Dennis Haysbert played a U.S. president in the TV series "24."
- King George VI suffered from a bad stutter, which was most pronounced when he delivered public speeches.
- Stewart says a lot of swear words that get bleeped out on TV.

Life After Laughs

- Pee-Yew Research Center sounds like Pew Research Center.

Composition Theorist Parodies

- Thank you to **Fabio Fantini** for designing this graphic.

Edifying the Heads of the Student Body by Means of Application of the Romance Languages as a Didactic Discipline of the Composition of the English Tongue

- Peter Elbow (not Ankle) is a well-known composition theorist. He writes verbosely about English composition theory, practice, process and teaching.
- Elbow is an advocate of "free writing," which essentially means writing without stopping. Elbow wrote *Writing with Power* (not *Writing with Flour*).
- He taught feedback techniques he named "reader based" and "criterion based." Criterion based feedback judges the writing against standards. Reader based feedback judges the writing as perceived by readers.
- Patricia Bizzell (not Gizzard) is a composition theorist from the College of the Holy Cross (not the Bowl in Sauce) in Worcester (like Worcestershire Sauce), Massachusetts.
- Rosetta Stone is a foreign language learning software program.
- Elbow wrote *Writing without Teachers* (not *Writing without Bleachers*).
- Elbow and fellow composition theorist David Bartholomae (not Barfholomae) had a contentious public disagreement. Elbow argued that writing comes from the individual and Bartholomae argued that a writer must prove himself or herself first. Elbow maintains that writers should be accepted from the beginning. Bartholomae contends that a writer cannot learn without a teacher.
- Elbow wrote *The Believing Game* (not *Believing in Q-Bert*).
- "Jeux sans frontieres" means "Games without borders" in French.
- Elbow wrote *The Uses of Binary Thinking* (not *The Uses of Binary Fingers*).
- Elbow wrote *The Music of Form* (not *The Music of Porn*).
- Elbow wrote *Coming to See Myself as a Vernacular Intellectual* (not *Coming to Manhood as a Vernacular Intellectual*).
- Elbow and Bartholomae co-authored *Responses to Bartholomae and Elbow* (not *Responses to the Chicken and Egg Debate*).
- Elbow wrote *Should We Invite Students to Write in Home Languages? Complicating the Yes/No Debate* (not *Should We Invite Students into Our Homes? Complicating the Yes/No Debate*).

Make No Room for Kids: Bells Ding for Online Classes K-8: An Argumentative Abstract by Richard Fukerson

- Richard Fulkerson (not Fukerson) is a composition theorist and instructor of English.
- Harlequin Frogs are endangered.
- Stony Lane Elementary School and The Good Shepherd School are real.
- James Berlin (not James Irving Berlin) wrote *Rhetoric and Ideology in the Writing Class* (not *Rhetoric and Climatology in the Writing Class*).

Extrapolating the Fundamentals of Dexterous English Composition by Tutelagical Virtue, Endemic to Asian Languages and Chinese Symbolism

- Lawrence A. Cremin (not Cretin) was an educational historian.
- Avery Coonley School for Gifted Children is a real school.
- James Berlin (not Berlint)—another theorist—wrote about creating a "safe" writing environment during the Cold War. Berlin wrote *The Politics of Historiography* (not *The Politics of Histrionicgraphy*).
- Peter Elbow wrote *How to Enhance Learning by Using High-Stakes and Low-Stakes in Writing* (not *How to Enhance Yearning by Using Pork Steaks and Beef-Steaks in Writing*).
- In References, Chinese translations: 未知 means "Unknown." "這一狗狗世。" means "It's a dog eat dog world." "中青年誌" means "Chinese Journal of Adolescents."
- Irving Berlin wrote the song "There's No Business Like Show Business."
- Bartholomae wrote *Writing on the Margins: Essays on Composition and Teaching* (not *Writing on the Margarine: A Composition Cookbook*).
- The founder of electrochemistry was Sir Humphry (not Humpty) Davy. He was mentored by Quaker businessman Robert Dunkin.

Bad Ass Drafts

- Anne Lamott (not Anne Lamott Applesauce) wrote *Bird by Bird: Some Instructions on Writing and Life* (not *Tail by Tail: Some Instructions on Writing and Vibes*).
- Lamott's most known chapter in this book is called "Shitty First Drafts" not "Bad Ass Drafts." "Bad Ass Drafts" parodies the entire "Shitty First Drafts" chapter.
- These are some REAL quotes from Lamott's "Shitty First Drafts" from her book *Bird by Bird: Some Instructions on Writing and Life*. (Random House Books, 1995):

    "...people think that they [successful writers] sit down at their desks every morning feeling like a million dollars...they take in a few deep breaths, push back their sleeves, roll their necks a few times to get all the cricks out, and dive in."

    "[Good writers] do not find themselves bounding along like Huskies across the snow."

    "I mentioned this to my priest friend, Tom. He said you can safely assume you've created God in your image when it turns out God hates all of the same people you do."

    "If one of your characters wants to say 'Well, so what Mr. Poopy Pants,' you let her."

    "I used to write food reviews for *California Magazine* before it folded. (My writing reviews had nothing to do with the magazine folding, although...some readers took umbrage at my comparing mounds of vegetable puree with various ex-presidents' brains.)"

    "...I mentioned this [her writing experience] to a hypnotist I saw...at first I thought he was feeling around on the ground for some silent alarm button."

    "A writer friend of mine suggests opening the jar and shooting them [imaginary mice that represent your family and other human beings] in the head. But I think he's a little angry, and [last line] I'm sure nothing like this would ever occur to you."
- In "Shitty Drafts" Lamott writes jocularly about "Charles Manson girls" and shooting up.
- Lad Tobin is a composition theorist who wrote *Reading Students, Reading Ourselves: Revising the Teacher's Role in the Writing Class* (not *Eating Students, Eating Ourselves: Digesting the Teacher's Role in the Writing Class*).
- Fulkerson refers to Elbow as "Aristotle in modern dress" in his essay *Four Theories of Composition*.
- 3157 E. Elmwood, 85034 is the mailing address for University of Phoenix.

Whimsor College breaks earth in 2015. Whimsor is an imaginary liberal arts college, wherein wacky, wonderful students and teachers take place.

Whimsor is nestled inside the Wilshire Woods in Columbia, Missouri. This fictitious institution of higher learning is a mere two miles north of the city center—North of Shady Lake and East of Bear Creek Trail.

Featuring: *Grade A Papers II: A funny coffee table book for HISTORY teachers and the Universe*

About the author

Elizabeth Schaefer is a new humorist and creator of Books on a Whim (dreamed up May 24, 2013 and incorporated July 23, 2013).

In addition to writing humorous books on a whim, Elizabeth is currently completing a graduate program in Written Communication with the goal of fulfilling her dream of being a college English teacher.

- May 2014

Books on a Whim, Inc.
Booksonawhim.com
info@booksonwhim.com
P.O. Box 5066
Evanston, IL   60204-5066

Papers draw blanks without design.
Donate to "Grade A Art" at booksonawhim.com/design.html.
Donations will print you dedications in the next Grade A Papers book!

www.ingramcontent.com/pod-product-compliance
Lightning Source LLC
Chambersburg PA
CBHW040905020526
44114CB00037B/63